WHY ME?

UNTOLD TRUTHS ABOUT LIFE

DENNIS AMANKWAH

ISBN: 978-9988-53-480-6

To sponsor or share your testimonies, kindly contact **+233 (0) 540688684** or email at dennisamankwah36@gmail.com. Join my **Facebook** page **(https://www.facebook.com/DACreateYourOw nLife/)**, or follow me Twitter **(@DennisAmankwa13)** for more updates about future books from me.

Cover design by Dennis Amankwah. Cover image by Pexels/Pixabay

DEDICATION

To the curious many who seek meaning and understanding to life's challenges.

CONTENTS

ACKNOWLEDGMENTS

Special thanks to God for the opportunity accorded me to put down these ideas into a book, so I can share with you. It has been a lovely journey of rediscovery over these past years.

A thank you to my launch team, in the persons of Derick Kojo Howard, Prince Noble Allah, Stephen Ofori and finally Rebecca Nartey, for their support throughout the whole book launch period. It has been wonderful working with you guys. Thank you so much.

To Collins Gogoe Quesi Adoko, Derrick Howard and Stephen Ofori, thank you once again for critiquing the manuscript. I really appreciate your immeasurable contributions and efforts.

To you, my reader, thank you for picking up this book to read. I hope this book be a blessing to you and your loved ones, to help you understand life's challenges and how you can live a fulfilling life accordingly.

INTRODUCTION

THE STORY BEHIND THE WRITING OF THIS BOOK

The year 2010 to 2015 was the darkest moments of my life, with a peak occurring around 2013. It was a hell lot of moments for me. I never even thought I could survive. Many times, I entertained suicidal thoughts but I just couldn't find good reasons to commit one. Now I think one of the reasons why I couldn't really commit suicide was that I could live to tell the tale of my quest and the outcomes thereof; to share with you what I found in my quest to understand why I was going through those challenging moments. If I am to factor in the illusion of time and the eternal moment of Now concept (which is later explained in the book), then I can say that this present me knew before time that at this moment, I would want to author a book by name "Why Me? Untold Truths About Life". So, my spirit-soul, which is all knowing, arranged for my past self (2010 to 2015) to go through hell so that I can gain the necessary experiences and knowledge to write this book.

Fast forward to 2019/2020, I can look back and say that indeed all things were working together for my good and, for my becoming. My understanding of life and the challenges thereof has been enriched by virtue of the experiences I went through. It was hell though but it was worth it. And that is something I want to share with you through this book, so that perhaps you can also be enlightened about this whole journey of life on Earth. The idea for writing this book was conceived in 2013 but I couldn't really write then, the challenging moments didn't give the clarity to write. But in 2019, the idea to write on this same topic came again. I gave it a go and that has resulted in the making of this book. As the title suggest, I try to answer the question 'Why Me?', a question almost every one of us asks, in times of difficulties, when life's events don't make any sense or meaning to us. And I try to approach the answer to the question from the spiritual, quantum physics, cognitive psychology, epigenetics, as well as nature's perspective. You will find the book quite interesting to read, approaching the question and answer from the spiritual, scientific and nature's points of view.

This is a three-part book where the first part talks about life from the beginning, what really is human life all about and the illusions of life. Part 2 deals with the reasons behind our life experiences especially the negative ones, from the spiritual, scientific and nature's perspective. You will learn of the spirit-soul's journey or path of evolution, the observer effect; how our belief systems and emotions influence the outcome of our lives. Part 3 addresses why it should be you and not someone else to go through what you are going through and how all things are working together for your becoming.

One of the challenges when writing this book was me trying to translate very complex scientific findings in common everyday language so that the average person can still read and understand. I tried my best to use common language and illustrations to explain the scientific findings while maintaining the integrity of those research outcomes. Part 1 of the book is a bit deep with scientific knowledge. I know that not everyone will have a full understanding of this part but kindly stick with reading to the end and you will appreciate and understand the whole book.

More so, though a pastor, I didn't have the intention of writing this book solely to the Christian community. I wrote it in such a way that any person of any religion can pick up the book to read and gain enlightenment from. The reason is that, life with its challenges haven't got anything to do with which religion you are affiliated with. So, there may be some terms and ideologies that may not necessarily agree to your belief systems. Nevertheless, if you will be patient and open-minded enough in reading this book, you will receive a lot of insights from this book; an immeasurable value to add to your life.

May this book be a source of light to illuminate your path in times of darkness. May you gain enlightenment to help face all life challenges with triumph and a smile, knowing very well that nothing in this life really matters and that nothing can really hurt you; the spirit-soul.

Dennis Amankwah
February 19, 2020.

14

PART 1

Intentionally left blank

The Beginning

"The universe is so unique and perfect that it could not have originated by chance but was divined by flawless, creative design."
~ Fritz Zwicky

When did all this begin; the thing we call Life? From whence did we come and where exactly are we going with Life? This and many more questions have plagued humanity for centuries; from science to religion to philosophy. We have been searching the earth, deep within it for answers. We have gone beyond our planet for answers. It is like a part of us wants to know what it is we are doing on Earth as human beings, the curious part of us that never ceases to ask these sorts of questions. Individuals from different ages have shared their insight on this. Many philosophers have likewise contributed their understanding to this quest of finding out what exactly we are doing on earth. Our scientific community has also contributed immensely to our understanding of life and what it is, in their own way of expression.

With all these immense contributions from different sources, of what life is, we are still not satisfied with ourselves. Something in us tells us that, there is more to life than we can imagine or write about in our philosophical books. And indeed, life is more than any of us can write or read about. To understand whence we came from and where we are going with life, let's first look at what happened at the beginning or before time as we know and understand, began. For a more scientific interpretation of time and the beginning of the universe, my readers can refer to *The Universe in a Nutshell* and *A Brief History of Time* by Stephen Hawking. He has an interesting representation of the universe and its beginning from the scientific perspective.

Now back to us, what happened to initiate the beginning of the universe or time from a different perspective other than science? Cosmologists with their measurement of background microwave energy of the universe stipulate that the universe began with a big bang. Our different religions also agree to it that a Supreme Being, God, Allah, Brahman, etc. created the universe. This is the one common thing among all the different religions on Earth. Neither of these two opposing views of science and religion or spirituality is wrong. Both are expressing what happened in their own ways and understanding. The truth is science cannot explain every happenings of the universe neither can religion explain every occurrence. So, both views are needed to complement one another.

'The Big Bang Theory is the leading explanation about how the universe began. At its simplest, it says the universe as

we know it started with a small singularity, then inflated over the next 13.8 billion years to the cosmos that we know today."
~ Elizabeth Howell, what is the Big Bang Theory.

Science and religion or spirituality can only speak of what happened at the beginning. But what really happened before time itself began; before the universe and everything in it came into existence? To understand this question let us infer from the two polarizing views of the universe and its beginning. From both science and religion, it can be deduced that the universe as it appears to us today came out of nothing. That is, before time began or the universe began, there was absolutely nothing. Nothing existed. Then out of nothing (no-thing) came everything that we see and interact with today. This 'no-thing' is what has been referred to by scientists as the energy that caused the big bang and hence the beginning of the universe.

'No-thing' has been referred to by many names across our different religions. Some refer to it as God, Goddess. Others call it Allah or Brahman, etc. It has many names across many cultures and societies on Earth. Yet it is 'no-thing'. Science refers to this 'no-thing' as energy and the religious folks refer to it as God or Supreme Being. Interestingly, both references carry the same or similar definition.

In its simplest form, energy is defined by scientists as that which cannot be created or destroyed but can transform or be transformed from one state to another. Religion defines God or Supreme Being as that which was neither created and cannot be destroyed. Religion says that God is omnipresent; present in all matter. Science says energy is present in all matter and antimatter; energy is present everywhere. So, the scientist who says the universe is full of energy is no different from the religious person who says the universe is full of God, Allah or Supreme Being. They are both expressing the same thing (no-thing) in different diction.

"By faith we understand that the universe was formed at God's command, so that what is seen was not made out of what was visible"
Hebrews 11:3, NIV.

Let's see how it all began from a different perspective. One celestial moment, 'no-thing' which had some form of consciousness or awareness to itself, realized that it knew all knowledge of all it was. Yet, it had not experienced all the knowledge it knew of itself. [1]*Note that recent development in science and our understanding of the universe points to the fact that the universe is not a dead something as we thought some centuries back. Current scientific evidence suggests that the universe is alive or have some form of consciousness to itself. It somehow knows of its existence and its role in creating and supporting life.* So, for 'no-thing' to experience all of its knowledge, it decided to split itself into infinite selves so that each self will experience part of the knowledge of the whole 'no-thing'. The force with which this creative event took place is what scientists may refer to as the big bang. It was a supermassive energy transaction that kick start time as we have come to know it.

The creation of time was necessary so that each experience of the infinite selves of 'no-thing' would be compared to or related with it. In fact, every experience we have as humans is always in relation to something, time or otherwise. After this supermassive energy transaction, some selves of 'no-thing' decided to turn into planets like the Earth; to host other selves of the same 'no-thing' like the trees, animals, water, air, humans, etc. Some selves of this same force formed into stars like our Sun; to give light to the planets. Some formed into evil or demonic beings so that the rest of the other selves of 'no-thing' can distinguish between good and evil. This is because there cannot be good if there's no evil. If there's no evil then we cannot know that which is good from that which is evil. Some formed into angelic beings to guide the ways of the "younger" selves of 'no-thing' that have also begun the process of experiencing the no-thingness in themselves.

> *"God does not play dice with the universe; He plays an ineffable game of His own devising, which might be compared, from the perspective of the players, (i.e. everybody), to being involved in an obscure and complex version of poker in a pitch-dark room, with blank cards, for infinite stakes, with a Dealer who won't tell you the rules, and who smiles all the time."*
> *~ Neil Gaiman.*

'No-thing' created infinite versions of itself so that each self will experience the infinite knowledge of 'no-thing' in its own unique way. The Sun, for example, is experiencing the infinite knowledge in its own way by shinning on us. We as humans also experience this same infinite knowledge by basking in the Sun and using the sun's energy for other things. Every aspect of this Infinite Source, experiences some form of this Source in its own unique way.

[2]This creation process is an ongoing event, contrary to the popular Christian belief that God rested on the seventh day after creating the universe. 13.8 billion years have passed since this whole process began, spinning out galaxies, planets, stars, moons, sentient beings like we humans, etc. And even as I type this, new galaxies, stars, planets, etc. are forming in our universe. After all the infinite selves of 'no-thing' have come to the fullness of the knowledge of 'no-thing', all shall then return to the 'no-thing' state again. Then the whole process of life or creation will begin all over again.

For now, we don't know exactly when this event of everything returning to the first singularity point will occur. But cosmologically speaking, the universe will definitely shrink on itself somewhere in the far distant future, to the one single point or moment that began it. For now, the universe is expanding and expanding at a rapid rate than ever estimated and it will keep on expanding for some millions, billions or probably trillions of years to come. But eventually, the energy responsible for this expansion will run out and when it does, the reverse reaction will kick in, causing the universe and everything in it to shrink on itself to one single moment of nothingness.

"The reason why the universe is eternal is that it does not live for itself; it gives life to others as it transforms."
~ Lao Tzu

And thus, began you and I. From this same 'no-thing we all sprung, just to experience what it is to be part of the nothingness. And thus, began life as we have come to know it. Don't be offended in any way that I have referred to your God as 'no-thing'. Because that is exactly what it is? God is not a thing. And if God is not a thing, then God is nothing (no-thing).

"The universe is a machine where you have been placed, and like a machine the outcome can be known. Every battle has already been won or lost. All that is left is for you to choose your side."
~ Unknown.

Life: What Is It?

"A happy life is one which is in accordance with its own nature."
~ Seneca.

Life has many and varied meanings to all the infinite selves of that which we call God or Supreme Being. Life to the Sun means giving off heat and light constantly and relentlessly to the planets and heavenly bodies that orbit it. Life to the moon means moving around the Earth and reflecting light from the Sun to the Earth all the days of its existence. Life will definitely have different meanings to all the infinite selves of the no-thingness.

Assuming our Sun, moon or even our planet Earth were self-conscious like we humans are, its meaning or definition of life will be entirely different from our definition of life. Interestingly, recent scientific findings suggest that it is not only us who possess consciousness to know or be aware of our existence in the universe but the universe as a whole possess some form of consciousness to it. The Earth somewhat knows of its existence and its purpose in hosting other life forms. The stars, moons, asteroids, etc. know in their own unique way that they exist and have a role or purpose to play in the universe.

"The Sun, with all the planets revolving around it, and depending on it, can still ripen a bunch of grapes as though it had nothing else in the Universe to do."
~ Galileo Galilee.

Life: From Human Perspective

"The universe is full of magical things, patiently waiting for our wits to grow sharper."
~ Eden Phillpotts.

What is life to us as humans; as sentient beings? This is a very difficult question to answer, in that, out of over 7 billion world human population, we can have 7 billion different definitions or meaning of life. Each person may have his or her own definition of life. To one, life may mean sufferings, difficulties and hardships. To another, life may be hassling and fighting for dominance. To others still, life may mean peace and tranquility, prosperity and wellbeing. But there can be one definition of life to sum all the individual definitions or meanings.

Thus, life can be defined as experiential moments in space-time continuum. What do I mean by experiential moment in space-time? No matter our individualized or personalized definitions of life, we all are experiencing the knowledge of who we are in the grand no-thingness. Whether it be love, fear, hatred, anger, suffering, peace, kindness, etc., they are all stuffs we feel or experience as part of the Divine Self.

The Divine Self or God gets to experience itself through our individual and collective experiences. I know this may be quite difficult for some to comprehend but think of it this way. You know intuitively that you are a father or mother, or you have some inner parental qualities. But until you give birth or adopt a child and go through the fatherhood or motherhood moments, you wouldn't be able to express the knowledge as a parent or you wouldn't experience what it is to be a father or mother. So, until the child comes up, what you may have will just be the knowledge, and not the experience of motherhood or fatherhood. Once the child comes on board, you begin to express yourself as a mother or father. Hence, you live life as a father or mother to your child or children.

> *"Change is at the very core of evolution and without it, all creatures would look alike and behave the same way."*
> *~ Martin Dansky.*

Life is an evolutionary process or moment in space-time continuum. We humans, alongside everything in this universe is evolving from one level of complexity to another. From the earliest humans that appeared on earth till now, we have observed changes to ourselves on all levels. Our early ancestors used to gather fruits, hunt with bare hands, etc. They later evolved to hunting with sharpened stones as weapons and learned to plant their own crops instead of hunting for foodstuffs. We have evolved from sleeping under the naked night sky to building huge mansions and skyscrapers. We have evolved from one form of complexity to another. And we are not yet done with our evolution process. As we evolve everything around us also evolve in their own pace. The moments of selfishness, anger, hatred, jealousy, envy, etc. that we experience are all part of the evolutionary process built into life by the great architect of life (God, Allah, Brahman, etc.).

By experiencing ourselves, we evolve or change from one state of being to another. Evolving from one level of awareness to another doesn't require only positive experiences. It requires both positive and negative experiences. Both positive and negative experiences have their role in what we become as sentient beings. One cannot exist without the other. Positive cannot exist without the negative and vice versa, as you will get to understand later on in this book.

"Change is inevitable. It is either you embrace it or become redundant."

In his book, *A Brief History of Time*, Stephen Hawking stated that the arrow of time, thermodynamics and cosmology all move in the same direction; the forward direction. The process of life as we have come to know it, is measured in time and with time. In other words, life has no option than to follow the arrow of time, i.e. to move in the forward direction. If life moves in the forward direction, then it means that the complexity of evolution increases with time in the same direction. Species of an organism become more and more complex or sophisticated as they grow from one generation to another.

Over time in the forward direction, we changed from cave dwellers to living in huge man-made buildings to travelling to space, etc. I can say that if we observe ourselves and nature, we get to understand that there is this inherent wisdom or intelligence in life that causes everything it is made of, to upgrade itself over time one way or the other. A design in nature that far exceeds our understanding and nothing in this universe can really resist this flow of energy or life.

Whenever we humans one way or another, resist this flow of energy, most often something catastrophic happens to us, which then forces us to change our ways and manners to align with what has happened. A classic example is our current issue of global warming. Out of greed and sheer will of dominance, we have been gradually destroying the very planet that sustains us. The Earth in its own way has been showing us signs of our impending doom if we continue on this path of destruction.

"The more clearly we can focus our attention on the wonders and realities of the universe about us, the less taste we shall have for destruction."

~ Rachael Carson

[3]The polar ices have been melting, increasing the volume of sea water and if this continues, somewhere in the near future most of our coastal cities and towns will be swallowed up by the monstrous sea we are creating. [4]Carbon dioxide concentration in the atmosphere reached all new high in May, 2019, over 400 ppm (part per million), the first time in the history of human beings. If we don't willfully change our ways to a more sustainable way of living on earth, sooner or later, something catastrophic will happen to us either to end our civilization on Earth or reduce our population drastically.

Understand that I am not a prophet of doom but when we continuously destroy the very thing that sustains our lives, we will be annihilated after the sustainer (the Earth) is destroyed by ourselves. We are oblivious to the fact that whatever part of the Earth we destroy; the air, land, water bodies, etc., we end up destroying ourselves. We are the earth. The food we eat, the air we breathe, the water we drink, are all derived from the Earth. When any part of the Earth is affected negatively by our insidious actions, we become negatively affected.

"Man is not, by nature, deserving of all that he wants. When we think that we are automatically entitled to something, that is when we start walking all over others to get it."
~ Criss Jami

Those who continue to resist this flow of life eventually become redundant and phase out of existence literally or metaphysically. A species that doesn't adapt to change, dies out gradually. A company that doesn't adapt to change in its timeline gradually phases out of existence. For example, as the race for electric vehicle (EV) increases, any major automobile company that doesn't adapt to the change but still stick to the production of hydrocarbon fuel vehicles will phase out of existence over time, maybe twenty to fifty years to come. Any relationship or marriage that doesn't adapt to change as it progresses, gradually loses its essence and phase out of existence. This is an entire cosmic event occurring at all levels of consciousness; in our individual lives, nature, industries, etc.

This may be what has commonly been referred to as 'survival of the fittest'. This phenomenon is not about who is strong or fit in a society. It is about adapting to change and the group that adapts eventually gets to survive. What has evolution got to do with my life? You may be wondering! The truth is everything including you in this universe evolves and I believe approaching life and the why question from this point of view can help us understanding what it is we are doing on Earth and how we can live a more fulfilling and stress-free life. So, stay with me as we try to understand 'why me?' a question almost everyone asks himself or herself whenever life experiences become tough and unbearable.

"Evolution is not a force but a process. Not a cause but a law."
~ John Morley

Forms of Evolution

"It is not the strongest of the species that survives, nor the most intelligent that survives. It is the one that is the most adaptable to change."
~ Charles Darwin

Charles Darwin is known for his immense contribution to evolution. He did an astounding job observing nature and coming out with this law. Nevertheless, Darwinian evolution is limited somewhat to the physicals. It doesn't go beyond what exists in the material world. Evolution is far more complex and intriguing than Darwin could write about. Evolution transcends the physical into the metaphysical, spiritual or quantum world. Every level of the universe whether physical or non-physical undergoes some form of evolution from one state of being to another. The universe itself is evolving, so does everything in it. Evolution is at the center of the universe. Nothing escapes it in the long run. We as humans are no exception. Our bodies have evolved over thousands, probably millions of years, and continues to evolve as we progress through life. Aside our bodies evolving, our consciousness (spirit/soul) has been evolving over our stay on Earth.

The current state of the human spirit is entirely different from that of some five thousand years ago. Five thousand years ago, humans couldn't invent things like space travel, artificial intelligence, etc. As of this writing, we are thinking and talking about establishing human bases on the moon, Mars, etc. We just don't want to end with establishing human residence on our moon and planets in our solar system. We are thinking of inter-galactic space travel; building hypersonic spaceships that will allow traveling from our Milky Way galaxy to other galaxies faster and more efficient. That is the capacity of the human spirit as it evolves from one level of awareness to another. And I know that somewhere in a near or distant future, inter-galactic space travel and other highly advanced technologies will be easily available and accessible to the general human populace. This is because the more we advance in our evolution, the more we get to know and understand of the magnitude of the human spirit. The more aware we become of our true nature as gods, the greater feats we can accomplish.

> *"The cosmos is within us. We are made of star-stuff. We are a way for the universe to know itself."*
> *~ Carl Sagan.*

There are two forms of evolution; physical and non-physical (in the case of humans, consciousness evolution). For the purpose of this book, we will focus on the evolution of our consciousness (spirit-soul) and how it relates to why things happen to us as individuals and as a race of people. In chapter 1, we learnt that life is an experiential moment. To experience life in the physical sense, we leave the quantum world or spiritual world and pick up bodies in the form of babies to enable us make contact with the physical world. Once we come to this earthly world as babies, our spirits-souls use this opportunity to learn and unlearn itself of its true nature. As we grow from childhood to adulthood and finally die, we pick up certain characteristics or qualities of the soul and drop certain qualities whether good or otherwise. These characteristics shape our spirit-soul as it journeys through the physical world.

The state of an individual's spirit-soul evolution at birth and through his or her lifetime will determine how good or evil that person becomes and to a degree what that individual experiences in his or her life. The spirit-soul uses different life forms and different lifetimes to advance itself in its evolutionary process. There are two sides of the spirit-soul evolutionary spectrum; the negative and the positive sides. Each side of the spectrum is necessary for the spirit-soul to experience itself in the grand no-thingness. Without the negative, there cannot be the positive and vice versa. We can only tell of positive experiences because there are negative experiences. Without the other, we can't distinguish one from the other.

"… I have set before you this day life and good, and death and evil."
Deuteronomy 30:15, KJV.

Evolutionary Paths

'Each one of us has our own evolution of life, and each one of us goes through different tests which are unique and

challenging. But certain things are common. And we do learn things from each other's experience. On a spiritual journey, we all have the same destination."
~ A. R. Rahman.

A spirit-soul can decide to start its evolution process from the negative spectrum of life experiences. An individual with such spirit-soul can go through a lot of negative experiences naturally. It is either this person suffers a lot at the hands of people or does a lot of harm or damage to other people or both. This may occur in a single lifetime or many lifetimes of that particular spirit-soul. Once that spirit-soul has experienced enough of negativity, it can decide to progress to the positive spectrum of life events in same lifetime or separate lifetimes or can sometimes become lost in its negativity for a moment. Another spirit-soul being can decide to start its evolutionary path from the positive spectrum towards the negative spectrum of life and back to the positive spectrum.

Why should a spirit-soul decide to experience negativity if it can choose to positive experiential moments in its lifetime? Well, remember life is an experiential moment; moments in time to experience the no-thingness in ourselves. And these experiential moments include both negative and positive ones. The architect of life designed it in such a way that all selves of 'Itself' have some form of free will to themselves to choose whichever form of experience to have, whether positive or negative.

Whichever path of evolution a spirit-soul chooses in its lifetime, it attracts equivalent spirit-souls or spirit-souls vibrating in the same plane to itself. These like-minded entities help and contribute to the evolution of the said spirit-soul. A person traveling on the negative frequency of life experience will attract spirit-soul individuals or entities vibrating on the same negative frequency, so that they can evolve together. Likewise, a spirit-soul individual who decides to travel on the positive frequency of life. This can be said in layman's term as birds of a feather flock together. This saying doesn't just apply to physicality, it also applies to spirituality. An evil individual can have a few or hordes of evil entities about himself or herself that he or she may not be aware of. Likewise, a benevolent person will have some hosts of similar spiritual entities about himself or herself. Whichever side of the spectrum one finds himself or herself, there are hosts of individuals and entities available to assist that spirit-soul.

"New age values are conscious evolution, a non-sectarian society, a non-military culture, global sharing, healing the environment, sustainable economies, self-determination, social justice, economic empowerment of the poor, love, compassion in action, going beyond religious fundamentalism, going beyond nationalism-extreme nationalism."
~ Deepak Chopra.

This body-soul-spirit evolutionary path is quite an intricate process. Every decision whether springing from the body or the spirit-soul affects one another. That is, decisions made by the spirit-soul of an individual affects the physicality of that person and any decision made from the physical point of view likewise affects the spirit-soul of the individual. Moreover, whatever decision an individual makes whether good or otherwise affects not just himself or herself but everything in the universe. This is because as we evolve, the Earth, the Sun, our galaxy, the entire universe evolves with us and through us; our actions and choices. Everything is interconnected and intertwined with one another. And there's a lot of scientific researches to suggest that we are electromagnetically connected to everyone and everything around us. This means our thoughts, words and actions affect one another on a microscopic (quantum) level and also on a macro-scale level. Most times, the effect of our actions and decisions are so subtle that we don't recognize its immediate impact on people and things around us. All these affect our body-soul-spirit evolution.

As a Ghanaian, my decisions and actions contribute to the development of my body-soul-spirit. These decisions and actions of mine in turn contribute to the development of the Ghanaian spirit-soul. This then influences the African spirit and finally the global human spirit. The evolutionary path of the spirit-soul starts its journey from the individual to the community to the nation, then the continent and finally the whole world. Likewise, any person of any nationality. We all contribute to our individual evolution, that of our nations, continents and the whole world wide.

That's why it is so popular to hear people say that if you want to change the world to make it a better place, you first start with yourself. This is because the individual selves make the collective global selves and the global human spirit-soul cannot be made whole if the individual spirit-souls have not been made whole. Our numerous religions on Earth also contribute to our individual and collective spirit-soul evolution. The Muslim is contributing to the evolution of the Islamic spirit, likewise the Christian, Buddhist, etc. As a Christian or any religious person evolves, it is not just his or her spirit-soul that evolves. The Christian community spirit evolves as well or the religion of the person evolves as well.

"Our greatest human adventure is the evolution of consciousness. We are in this life to enlarge the soul, liberate the spirit, and light up the brain."
~ Tom Robbins.

Who can know the evolutionary path of a spirit-soul? No one can tell exactly the path of a spirit-soul, save the spirit-soul of the individual and the Grand Architect of life, aka God, Allah, etc. It is very important to understand this, so that we can appreciate the complexity of life and all that it has got to offer us. Try as much as possible not to ridicule, pity or judge any individual for the afflictions he or she may be going through. It is very likely that, that is what the spirit-soul has chosen in such lifetime to experience. Instead of ridiculing or judging people, we should rather show compassion towards one another and towards the afflicted.

Compassion is rooted in love and only love can heal and mend the wounds of the spirit-soul. Compassion can help the spirit-soul to remember that it has all the power and capacity to end the afflictions. It is not our place to judge others for who they are and who they are not or who they choose to be. Judging and condemning others for what they have chosen to experience doesn't help. It only adds to the already exiting negativity and we can only overcome the negativity in this world by our positive synergy of love. The world has had enough of the negative energies and we must balance it out with positive energies like empathy, compassion, love, etc.

"Now these three abide; faith, hope and love but the greatest
of these is love."
1 Corinthians 13:13

The greatest gift we can give to a spirit-soul that is on the negative spectrum of evolution is love. Only pure and authentic love can help a spirit-soul on its path to recovery from the negative experiences. So, let love lead. Without love, we all will be adding to the already existing negative energies and the more negative energies in the world, the more it will attract its equivalent spirit-soul individuals to contribute more to it. And the more this happens, the worse the human spirit experiences become. So irrespective of your religious affiliations, let love lead. For the human spirit-soul is capable of giving and receiving love without any external influences. Moreover, let's strive to understand one another as a people.

We are all the same from the biological point of view; the same or similar biological makeup. But we are not all the same from a spirit-soul evolution perspective. We all have different paths to evolution of our spirit-soul. Some spirit-soul individuals may share similar evolutionary path yet the intensity and level of experiences for these individuals may not be the same for each of them. Let us love one another, respect, and appreciate one another's individuality and diversity while we celebrate our own uniqueness. The mad man or woman on the street is not of any less importance than any sane person. That may be what the spirit-soul of the individual has chosen to experience in that particular lifetime. The best we can do is to show love to one another, even to the most 'undeserving' individual among us. Because we were all created in love and for love.

"We can actually accelerate the process through meditation, through loving actions, through compassion and sharing, through understanding the nature of the creative process in the universe and having a sense of connection to it. So, that's conscious evolution."
~ Deepak Chopra.

The Illusions of Life

"I have lived on the lip of insanity, wanting to know reasons, knocking on a door. It opens. I've been knocking from the inside."
~ Rumi.

Life and all there is to it, is but a dream; a waking dream. Life is a wakeful dream, a reality that isn't real but only appears to be real in our minds. Life is an illusion that only the Masters or the spirit-soul that has achieved mastery in its evolution process can exists beyond this illusion. An illusion that we together with the Supreme Being have created from the beginning of time, so that we can use this illusion to experience ourselves; who we are as *pure essence* or God (if you would like to call it so).

Why do I say life is an illusion; some kind of divine magic trick? Life on earth or any other planet is related to time. And time is an illusion; a stubbornly persistent illusion. Past, present and future are all mental constructs. That which we call past, present or future exists only in our minds. In *pure essence*, *consciousness* or spirituality there is no time. Past, present and future all exist as one moment. I know this is crazy to wrap one's mind around. But that is an absolute truth. Time or the measure of it only exists in our minds. So, if life is based on time and time isn't that real as we think it is, then there is only one conclusion to life; it isn't real as we think it is. I know this sounds somewhat counter-intuitive but it's actually true that life is not that real as we think it is.

"When you are absolutely dissatisfied with things as they are, only then do you go in search, only then do you start rising higher. Only then do you make the effort to pull yourself out of the mud."
~ *Osho.*

Have you ever dreamed before? I dream a lot. My dreams most times feel so real that it is only when I wake up that I am able to tell that it was all just a dream. So, assuming one day I don't wake up from my dreams but continue to dream on for eternity, I will definitely lose my sense of physical reality and perceive this dream state as something really real. Of course, such an incident will not happen. I am only using that to illustrate what life really is. Life is a dream state that doesn't require us to sleep before we can enter that state. We are in that dream state as long as we draw breathe. We have been in this state for over thousands of years as a race; progressing from one level of awareness to another over those years. [5]Over two thousand years ago, humans didn't have the awareness that we were capable of building space shuttles and establishing human base on Mars and our moon. But here we are, thinking of sending humans and building permanent residence on the moon by 2024. And we will continue to be in this dream state until we awake one moment to realize it's all but a dream. A lot of people are gradually waking up to this reality of life.

"When you look in the mirror, what do you see? Do you see the real you, or what you have been conditioned to believe is you? The two are so different. One is an infinite consciousness capable of being and creating whatever it chooses, the other is an illusion imprisoned by its own perceived and programmed limitations."
~ David Icke.

[6]Interestingly, scientists are coming around to the conclusion that there isn't much difference between the dreaming brain and the waking brain. They both employ the same brain organs for the same type of experiences. What this means is that the brain organs responsible for coordinating your waking life are activated when you find yourself in a dream during sleep. That is, same organs are responsible for both your wakeful life and dream-state life. For example, the brain organ responsible for vision or sight when you are awake, is equally activated when you dream and see things in your dreams. If you are the type that dreams, you will realize that dreams can be as real as a waking life event. I remember in one of my dreams one day, I touched someone's breast in the dream and it felt so real; the tenderness and the skin texture, etc. I woke up and I was like "man this is damn serious and so real". Don't get me wrong here but dreams can be quite interesting and fun to have. Sometimes

you wake up from a dream, you wish it never ended or that you could go back into it.

All these dream stuffs are to help you understand what I am trying to mean that life isn't that real as we think it is. We will all one day wake up from this wakeful dream state called life and we will appreciate the magnificence of it. For now, let us enjoy the illusions and delusions of it. When we eventually wake up, we will realize that we are the universe. We are the life-force that permeates everything in the universe. We are the alpha and the omega; the beginning and the end. We are the 'I AM THAT I AM'. We would say as Jesus Christ said, that "I and the Father are one". This is the absolute state of being; when we return to our oneness with the Spirit-force or God.

> *"We live in a fantasy world, a world of illusion. The great task in life is to find reality."*
> *~ Iris Murdoch.*

A lot of things make up life's illusions and I am going to attempt to write on just a couple of them, the ones I think them to be that necessary to write on, for the purpose of this book. The key concepts I am going to touch on are the illusion of time, life and death, and freewill. To me these are the main illusions of life. All the others can be categorized into these three concepts. [7]You can read more on the concepts of illusions of life from the eastern world perspective. A link is provided in the reference page of this part. It is important for us to gain knowledge and understanding, so that we can live our lives accordingly. What's the essence of these? In order to enjoy every moment of your life whether good or bad, knowing very well that all things are working together for your good and not to take life too seriously. When you understand what life is all about, you will enjoy every moment of it, expressing gratitude for every moment that passes your way. Because you know that every moment is meant to come your way so that you can experience the divine in you. No life experience is ever out of proportion with the grand plan of the universe. Every form of experience is worth it, even the bad and worse ones.

"What is life? A madness. What is life? An illusion, a shadow, a story. And the greatest good is little enough; for all life is a dream, and dreams themselves are only dreams."
~ Pedro Calderon de la Barca.

The Illusion of Time

"The distinction between the past, present and future is only a stubbornly persistent illusion."
~ Albert Einstein.

Time is an illusion. Our sense of past, present and future is merely a mental breakdown of eternal moment of now. Everything exists in the Now state. Our minds have found a way to break this eternal moment of Now into past, present and future. An experience we have had exist in our minds as past, an experience that is still happening exists in the present and that which is yet to happen is in the future. On one level of awareness, all of what we call as past, present, future exists as one moment. And in this one singular moment, all that has happened, is happening or will happen is indeed happening at the same moment. That is, past, present and future events are all happening at the same moment. In this eternal moment, time isn't separated or segregated into units as past, present, future. All events are happening at the same moment.

Scientifically speaking, between quantum physics and neuroscience, there exists the theory that our minds exist in another dimension; a dimension outside of time. The brain is structured and operates in time but our minds are not time-bound. What I mean by the mind isn't time bound is that it exists in all moment (past, present and future) at the same time. This is quite intricate to understand. I know this is crazy and mind boggling; you learning that past, present or the future is an illusion and yet you can still tell yesterday from today and today from tomorrow. You can tell yesterday from today because your brain performs a lot of computational analysis to arrive at the conclusion that yesterday and today are different in a measure of time. This computational analysis of the brain is so rapid that we can hardly feel it taking place in our brains. Over thousands of years, our brains have tricked itself into believing that the past, present, future are separate units of time in space-time continuum. [8]Read more on the mind and its connection to the brain via quantum entanglement and quantum tunneling the link provided in the reference section of Part 1.

"Your future self is watching you right now through memories, and your past self is hoping for you to succeed. Make yourself proud."
~TheLastHero7.

Let's use this scenario to help you understand more clearly what I am trying to mean here. The truth is this scenario that I am about to illustrate doesn't come close to representing the idea but let me use it anyway. Assume this eternal moment of now is like your favorite movie. Your favorite movie is made of fragments of images or pictures moving at a rapid rate, so fast that your brain perceives the images as a movie instead of single images. If the rate of the image movement is slowed, each frame of image can be taken out or replaced. Assuming each image is processed at a very slow rate, a single image can be perceived as a past, present or future moment depending on the order of the images. That is, at any moment of the slowed movie, you can single out one moment as past, present or future.

When your movie is playing at its normal rate, you view every scene as a single moment but in reality, that single moment is made up of a lot of individual frames of images. Those individual images constitute the single moment. So, think of this eternal moment of now as a single moment or scene in your favorite movie or any other movie, where all things are happening at the same time. And think of past, present, future as the individual images that make the single scene in your movie. As biological beings, our brains have not evolved to the point where it can perceive the flow of life's event as one single moment. Therefore, our brains break down this single moment into fragmented moments; what we have come to call as past, present, future. This is to help the brain not go whack and also to help us experience who we are. We have to keep track of our evolutionary progress and that can only happen when we have time to relate our experiences with.

"I have realized that the past and future are real illusions that they exist in the present, which is what there is and all there is."
~ Alan Watts.

Moreover, what makes time an illusion is that it isn't constant. Our sense of time is subject to a lot of things, the paramount of which is the observer; that is, you the person measuring time, and the object being observed. For example, on Earth our measure of time is relative to the position of the Earth from the Sun. The Earth revolves on its axis to give us day and night, and around the Sun to give us years. Assuming we found ourselves on any planet apart from Earth, our sense and measure of time will be different. Someone on planet Mars will have shorter day and night; 23 hours, 45 minutes of Earth time as compared to 24 hours on Earth.

This means, someone on Mars will experience shorter years than someone on Earth. Though a

Martian will not feel this change of time since all his or her biological makeup will be tuned to the movement of the planet and its relation to the Sun. So, time is relative and dependent on the observer. [9]For example, it takes 8 minutes 20 seconds for light to travel from the Sun to the Earth. Whiles someone on Earth will see the sun's light as something happening in the present moment, someone on the Sun will interpret the event as past. That is the sunlight on Earth is a past moment to the Sun but a present moment to the Earth, considering the packets or photons of light leaving the Sun's surface to Earth.

> *"It is not that we have little time, but more that we waste a good deal of it."*
> *~ Seneca*

Have you ever observed that there are some moments in the year, time appears to pass at a faster rate and at certain moments the passage of time is very slow? Have you become so engrossed in an activity that time seemed to pass at a fleeting moment? You enjoyed doing what you were doing so you lost count of the passing hours. By the time you realized, the day was all over. While you processed the moment as fleeting, someone across the globe or next to you processed it as being slow. This and many more make time as dependent on who is observing it. To one it is fast and to other it is slow. To one it is past, to another it is present or future. On a higher level of awareness or consciousness, all life's events are occurring at the same moment. There is no past, present or future. There's just one big single eternal moment of now; where everything that has ever happened is still happening and will continue to occur, world without end.

"The part of you that is unhampered by illusion-the illusion of time, the illusion of powerlessness, the illusion of impossibility- is waiting for you to slow down and open up so that it can speak to your consciousness. In some unguarded moment, you will hear its wildly improbable words and know that they are guiding you home."
~ Martha Beck.

Contrary to the popular assumption that our time is limited, we have infinite amount of time to experience ourselves. Experiencing who we are as gods or spiritual beings will require more than just one lifetime. As a fact, one lifetime of about 70 to 100 years age will not be enough to experience the grandness of the human spirit on individual levels. The spirit-soul has to keep coming back to the earthly realms to experience more of itself via independent bodies. Someone is asking, is this guy talking about reincarnation? Yes, I am talking about reincarnation. You may or may not believe in reincarnation and I am not asking you to believe in it if you have been raised not to. Nonetheless, it an event that happens and there are a lot of evidence to support it. Via reincarnation, the spirit-soul is able come back to the earthly realm to experience all of itself in all different ways. [10]You can find more about reincarnation researches in the reference section.

The saying that we all have one life to live is true only on the surface. This is because when I die as Dennis Amankwah, the lifetime of this me has ended, it doesn't necessarily mean the lifetime of the spirit-soul me has ended. What has ended is the physical me not the spirit-soul me. In a deep sense, we have more than just one life. After death, the spirit-soul leaves the earthly realm. Now if this spirit-soul hasn't completed its evolution cycle or has not achieved mastery yet, it can come back to the earthly realm as a new individual to continue its evolution. And it will keep coming until it reaches it evolution peak via human experiences. In fact, I can say that all of us living have lived multiple past lives to get us to this far, though most of us don't really remember any of our past lives. In part 3 of the book I will explain to you why most of us don't remember any of our past lives, from the scientific point of view.

"Don't grieve. Anything you lose comes around in another form."
~ Rumi.

This is basically because we have not evolved to the point where we can remember all or any of our past lives. Few people have had that awareness of having lived a past life somewhere. This forgetfulness of past lives is somewhat necessary so that we can experience each lifetime as something new and untainted by any past experiences whatsoever, yet continuous of our past lives.

I remember one day in my meditation, I was contemplating on the grandness of God and how I can get to experience all of it and it was ministered to my spirit-soul that I have infinity to learn of God so I should take my time to learn all I want to learn in this lifetime. Likewise, you and your spirit-soul have infinity to learn of yourself and God/Goddess. Our human spirit-soul is too magnificent for us all to learn of all of it in just one lifetime.

We have eternity to experience ourselves; the good and bad in all of us. I know this may sound counterintuitive to popular western religious views but in effect that is what it is. If we are to experience the fullness of the gods we are, logically it is going to take more than just seventy to one hundred years lifespan to do that. We will need thousands of years and since the human body cannot last beyond two hundred years, we have to keep coming back into new bodies or as new babies after our old bodies expire and die out.

> *"Time is basically an illusion created by the mind to aid in our sense of temporal presence in the vast ocean of space. Without the neurons to create a virtual perception of the past and the future based on all our experiences, there is no actual existence of the past and the future. All that there is, is the present."*
> *~ Abhijit Naskar, Love, God and Neurons: Memoir of a scientist who found himself by getting lost.*

The illusion of time is necessary so that our brains or minds can accommodate each experience and not become confused by all of them happening at the same time. Moreover, it is also necessary so that we can in a way measure the experiences we have and the progress we make on our evolutionary path. I know as we advance in our science and technology as a race, we will be able to develop the technology that can distort the space-time fabric around us, to enable us to either go into the past or the future in the flesh. And not just our consciousness travelling into the past or future via dreams, visions or some psychic phenomenon.

If we will understand life from this perspective, there wouldn't be room in our lives for guilt, shame, fear, anxiety, regrets. There wouldn't be regrets because we will understand that if by whatever means we are not able to accomplish any particular achievement in one lifetime; we can always come back after death (reincarnate) to accomplish whatever the spirit-soul desires. We wouldn't also rush through life; over stressing our bodies to incur stress related illnesses, thereby shortening our physical lifespan.

"What, if some day or night a demon were to steal after you into your loneliest loneliness and say to you: 'This life as you now live it and have lived it, you will have to live once more and innumerable times more'… Would you not throw yourself down and gnash your teeth and curse the demon who spoke thus? Or have you once experienced a tremendous moment when you would have answered him: 'You are a god and never have I heard anything more divine.'"
~ Friedrich Nietzsche.

We would move through life with the grace that no matter what, we will be alright. You see, the world and its systems teach us that we don't really have time. That we are limited by time. From the physical perspective, this may be true. But this doesn't hold true for our spirit-souls. Our spirit-souls abounds in infinity. So, reach deeper into yourself either through meditation, prayers or whatever method appeals to your faith, whenever you feel like you are out of time. Go deeper into yourself; to the place where you (spirit-soul) dwell. The higher place where there is no time. Reach into this timeless place in you for nourishment when the need arises.

If you can learn to slow yourself down and avoid rush hours or moments in your life, you will have peace with yourself. You will avoid stress related disorders and you can prolong your lifespan a few more years above the average human lifespan. While it is true that we can reincarnate, certain past experience cannot be repeated as we progress with our individual evolution. With every new life form that we pick on our journey back to Earth as new babies, we may never meet certain loved ones from our past lives. We will never get to enjoy certain pleasures. So, it is important that we treat each lifetime with dignity, love, etc. We have to enjoy very moment of our lives knowing very well that once those moments pass, we won't get them back. Don't listen to what the world is saying. Listen to what your spirit-soul is saying and if you do, you will enjoy life to its fullest even in your dark moments.

"Infuse your life with action. Don't wait for it to happen. Make it happen. Make your own future. Make your own hope. Make your own love. And whatever your beliefs, honor your creator, not by passively waiting for grace to come down from upon high, but by doing what you can to make grace happen… yourself, right now, right down here on Earth."
~ Bradley Whitford.

The Illusion of Death

"Learn to enjoy every minute of your life. Be happy now. Don't wait for something outside of yourself to make you happy in the future. Think how really precious is the time you have to spend, whether it's at work or with your family. Every minute should be enjoyed and savored.
~ Earl Nightingale.

Death! Something we fear to talk about. Yet it will happen to all of us. We are all going to die one day and none of us can escape its powers. The rich will die, so as the poor. The beggar will die, so will the giver of alms. Everybody will die one day whether he or she likes it or not. Of course, it is difficult making peace with death. Leaving behind our loved ones, our riches and vanities, etc. No one really wants to die. Yet there is very little we can do about death. We can find ways to prolong our lives for some few hundreds of years like learning of the immortality trick of jellyfishes yet we will eventually end up dying one day. We can learn to transfer our consciousness to machines or artificial bodies so that we can live forever like in sci-fi movies, which is highly unlikely but maybe possible in some thousands of years to come. Even if we are able to accomplish such a great achievement, we will likely grow weary of having to live for so long that we will desire for death one way or the other.

There is beauty in death, just like there is beauty in everything that has been created in the universe. Death occurs at all levels of creation, from the tiniest element to the super molecular structures. There is annihilation in atoms; the building blocks of matter. So, death is at the atomic level. Death is at the center of the universe, since all matter in the universe are made of atoms. We live in a universe where every matter in it will eventually end up dying no matter how long it takes.

There is beauty in death, if it is viewed from a love-based perspective than from a fear-based perspective. There should not be any reason for us to fear death if we understand from the perspective that nothing can really escape its power and that the real us (spirit-soul) doesn't die. And that death is necessary for our evolution processes whether physical or spiritual. Just like there cannot be light without darkness, there cannot be life without death. Everything exists in pairs. Light and darkness, good and bad, male and female, God and Satan (devil), hot and cold, etc.

> *"We all die. The goal isn't to live forever, the goal is to create something that will.*
> *~ Chuck Palahniuk.*

Let's approach death from a philosophical or scientific point of view. I believe it will help ease our pain and fear of death. All life is made up of energy. Energy, like God/Allah cannot be created but can be transformed from one form to another. In other words, life as an energy, can only be recycled and the only way this can happen is via death. After death, every organism returns to the Earth whatever energy it took from it. This energy goes into sustaining the ecosystem. And humans are no exception. The body we carry are not ours. It is a product of the Earth and as such will return to the Earth one day.

Through death, the life energy is renewed or recycled. The Earth itself will die one day. This is because, our planet depends on the Sun for life. What will happen when the Sun runs out of fuel to produce heat and light? Earth will gradually become cold and not able to sustain life on its surface. On the plus side, maybe by the time that the sun burns out and doesn't produce any heat and light, we would have evolved to the point that we can develop and build an artificial sun via nuclear fission technology and found a way to hang it in empty space to continue supplying light and heat to the planet. I don't know. Maybe. [11]As of this writing, we already have created or built artificial sun via nuclear fission reaction and on the process of perfecting it.

"Have you ever met someone for the first time, but in your heart, you feel as if you've met them before?"
~ JoAnne Kenrick, When a Mullo Loves a Woman

On the spiritual side or the spirit-soul evolution journey, every spirit-soul that enters the world as a new born baby brings with itself renewed energy from the spirit world. New born babies come to this world with fresh energy to renew the human spirit-soul experiences. This energy renewal is necessary for the continuity of the human spirit-soul evolution. Without this infuse of new spiritual energy by new born babies, the human evolutionary experiences can be stalled and die out over time. Nature wouldn't want the human race to go into extinction, therefore causes a man and a woman to be attracted to each other so that they can mate to produce children. Likewise, the spirit-soul wouldn't want an extinction level event in its evolution process, therefore will have to leave the body to the spirit world (die) at one time and return to pick new bodies (as new born babies) with fresh energy from the spirit world.

"It is not length of life, but depth of life."
~ Ralph Waldo Emerson.

Now this is the reason I say that death is also an illusion. We don't actually die. In my first book, 'Create Your Own Life', I explained that we are as God/Allah is. We are immortal or we share in the immortality of God/Allah. We don't die. Well, of course the body dies but we aren't the body. The body is more or less like a housing unit or a container for us to make contact with the material world. The real us, which is the spirit-soul living in our earthly body doesn't die. Our spirit-soul, which is our consciousness in one language, doesn't die. It cannot die because it is energy in its pure form and energy from its definition is something that cannot be destroyed.

[12]Evidence from scientific research suggests that in the first few moments after someone dies, consciousness (spirit-soul of the individual) is not annihilated or destroyed. As to where this consciousness goes after death is yet to be determined. There have been a lot of scientific researches into what happens to the spirit-soul after death and you can find more on the subject in the reference page of this part. The only reason why we don't appear to be like God is, is because we live in a body and living in a body comes with its limitations to the spirit-soul which is godlike.

> *"Death is not the opposite of life, but a part of it."*
> *~ Haruki Murakami.*

This is the beauty in death; that in it there is life. There cannot be the one without the other. Death gives us a richer perspective of what life is really all about. It humbles us. Even the most arrogant of us all, becomes humble on his or her death bed, when he or she knows that at such point nothing can be done to save their lives. Imagine a world where no one dies, with all our arrogance, stupidities, and vanities.

You can recall from the beginning of the chapter that life itself is an illusion. And if life and death go hand-in-hand like two eternal lovers, then death also is an illusion. It isn't real as we think it to be. Its reality only exists in our minds. If we are able to teach ourselves to move past our minds and the fear of death, we will realize that death is just another trick we are playing with ourselves. Through death, we can come back to the Earth to experience more and more of our spirit-soul. Only death can afford us that grace and convenience.

> *"To the well-organized mind, death is but the next great adventure."*
> *~ J. K. Rowling.*

The Illusion of Freewill

> *"Keep being the author of your own story. Never let anyone else write it for you again."*
> *~ Jennifer Donelly, Beauty and the Beast: Lost in a Book.*

Freewill! Do you we really have freewill? Some will argue that yes, we have freewill. Others will argue that no, we don't have freewill. Do we have freedom over the choices that we make and don't make? The answer is yes and no. To some level, we exercise freedom over the choices we make or don't make. But in reality, that is just another of life's illusions. On the surface, our choices may appear like there's some form of freedom to them but in reality, we are being run by some spiritual or divine software that has every choice we will ever make accounted for in its design. And there is nothing outside this spiritual code, though this code is boundless. No one knows the end or the beginning of this boundless or infinite choices. This infinity of choices is what we would call infinite possibilities. I know you will argue that, that is infinite choices and we have the freedom to choose any. Yes, on the surface we have that freedom but on a deeper level, no.

Think of it this way. Let's say you and I are like personal computers. Personal computers have operating systems that run them. Now, these computers cannot perform anything outside the operating system that runs them. That is, if you introduce a program not coded according to the operating systems running the computers. Within the operating system, the computers can perform infinite number of tasks. So, it's like within the operating system, there is some degree of freedom as to what the computers can do.

That freedom only exists within the boundaries of the operating system and within that system, we have infinite choices to make or not to make. In essence, we are like the computers and the energy (spirit-soul, God/Allah, etc.) that runs the universe is like the computer operating system. There is only some degree of freedom in this universal operating system (something I prefer to call as the Central Intelligence System (CIS)) to allow us write our own programs (destinies) out of it. This Central Intelligence System allows us to branch off to write our own codes (life experiences) out of it. All our individual codes (life experiences) whether good or otherwise are part of this CIS.

"Life is like a game of cards. The hand you are dealt is determinism; the way you play it is free will."
~ Jawaharlal Nehru.

Freewill is an illusion even on the physical level. There are tons of factors that affect the choices we make, though we claim to have freewill. Some of these factors we are conscious of, others we are not so aware of. Their workings are so subtle that we don't even realize that those things are influencing our choices. A classic example is couples falling in love. The choice of the man or woman is dependent on a lot of factors. Factors like the background which includes the home, society or community, nation, religion or non-religion, education, etc.

Even though, the man or woman has the freedom to choose any man or woman, these factors consciously or unconsciously influence the choice made or not made. Even nature plays a role in this kind of choice making. You think you like the man or woman with great or nice physiques and that is your free choice. No! You only appear to like them because your mind interprets men or women with great or nice physiques as highly reproductive. You may have your own rationalized reasons for falling in love but you can't beat nature to its reason for bringing a man and woman together; to foster the continuity of the human species through child bearing.

"There are only two kinds of people in the end: those who say to God, 'Thy will be done,' and those to whom God says, in the end, 'Thy will be done.'…"

~ *C. S. Lewis, The Great Divorce.*

Aside nature playing its tricks on us, our genes contain pieces of information that influences most of our decisions or choices. Information from our great grandparents, grandparents, parents are all lurking in our genes waiting for the right stimuli to go into operation. For example, assuming one's grandfather was a chronic alcoholic before the dad was born. That chronic alcoholism was encoded in his DNA, which was passed to the father. Assuming the father came to continue the legacy of drinking before the individual was born, such individual will also have the information to like alcoholic drinks, in his or her genes. And the very brief moments he or she get introduced to alcohol, the desire to get more of it becomes strong and with time, becomes alcoholic. Though on the surface it appears as if the individual made the choice to drink but in reality, he or she didn't. That decision to drink and become an alcoholic was largely influenced by his or her genetic compositions.

This in science is typically referred to as epigenetics. The study of heritable changes that do not involve alterations in the DNA sequence. In Christianity, it is termed as generational curse or so. Many of us think that we are living our lives; independent and of free will or choice. What we don't know is that some of our great grandparents if not all of them are still living and making choices through us. What I want to mean is, the baseline information in our genes that do subtly influence our decisions and choices do not originate from us but from our predecessors.

"Everything is determined, the beginning as well as the end, by forces over which we have no control. It is determined for the insect as well as the star. Human beings, vegetables, or cosmic dust, we all dance to a mysterious tune, intoned in the distance by an invisible piper."
~ Albert Einstein.

Even your decision to read this book was influenced by some previous conscious or unconscious decisions. That choice you made is like quantum entanglement. All our choices and decisions are entangled to almost everything in our past, present or future. Even the future decisions we have not made is entangled to the present choices we make or don't make. Quantum entanglement is defined as a physical phenomenon that occurs when pairs or groups of particles are generated, interact, or share spatial proximity in ways such that the quantum state of each particle cannot be described independently of the state of the others, even when the particles are separated by an infinite distance. What this long definition simply means is that, two particles no matter the distance between them whether billions of light-years away from each other, can still interact with each other instantly through some weird way.

Our choices or decisions which are made of energy which contains atoms or particles, behave in similar faction. Our thoughts and actions form an intricate web that interacts with every aspect of ourselves whether in the past, present or future. You think it's a free will decision you made. But if you are to analyze that decision critically, you will uncover almost all the underlining factors that influenced you to come to such conclusion. When you unearth the influential factors then you will realize that, that choice of yours hasn't got anything freewill to do with it.

> *"Man can do what he wills but he cannot will what he wills."*
> *~ Arthur Schopenhauer.*

In effect, freewill from both spiritual and physical point of view is an illusion. It isn't really real like life itself isn't real. It is something our brains or minds have conjured over its development, to give us some sense of control over our actions and inactions. We may have freedom to make any choice at all but we don't have the freewill, as in the power to act without the constraint of necessity or fate, or the ability to act at one's own discretion.

There are a lot of psychology and neuroscience experimental evidence that suggest that indeed freewill is just an illusion. Just like life and death, some things may be difficult for us to comprehend because of the conditioning of our minds over the years to believe certain things and not question them whether they be real or not. Life, death, freewill are all illusions whether we understand them or not, or believe them or not.

"In the mind there is no absolute or free will; but the mind is determined to wish this or that by a cause, which has also been determined by another cause, and this last by another cause, and so on to infinity."
~ *Baruch Spinoza.*

References

1. Hameroff S., Penrose R. (2014), "Consciousness in the Universe: A Review of the 'Orch OR' Theory", *Physics of Life Review*, Mar 11(1) pp 39-78.
2. End of the universe: https://www.youtube.com/watch?v=uD4izu DMUQA. Date accessed: April 2019.
3. : Polar ice melting: http://bit.ly/2XJExOm Date accessed: April 2019.
4. Carbon Dioxide Levels in Atmosphere hit Record High in May 2019: https://www.google.com/amp/s/phys.org/news/2019-06-carbon-dioxide-atmosphere-high.amp. Date accessed: June 2019.
5. NASA Moon to Mars in 2024: https://www.nasa.gov/topics/moon-to-mars Date Accessed: August 2019.
6. Human Brain and Dreams: https://www.theguardian.com/science/2017/apr/10/scientists-identify-parts-of-brain-in-dreaming Date accessed: August 2019.
7. Illusions of Life from Eastern World Perspective: https://chopra.com/articles/the-6-vedic-illusions-of-life-and-how-to-move-beyond-them Date accessed: August 2019.

8. The mind and its connection to the brain via Quantum Mechanics phenomenon: https://www.scienceandnonduality.com/article/a-new-theory-of-consciousness-the-mind-exists-as-a-field-connected-to-the-brain Date accessed: September 2019.

9. How long does it take sunlight to reach the Earth?: https://www.google.com/amp/s/phys.org/news/2013-04-sunlight-earth.amp Date accessed: September 2019.

10. Evidence of reincarnation: https://www.youtube.com/watch?v=S7SQoQj9868 Date accessed: January 2020.

11. Artificial Sun Technology: https://amp.scmp.com/news/china/science/article/3013431/chinas-artificial-sun-project-just-got-whole-lot-hotter Date accessed: June 2019.

12. What happens to the spirit-soul after death: https://www.soulproof.com/documented-evidence/ Date accessed: July 2019.

PART 2

Intentionally left blank

Why Do Bad Things Happen To Us?

"A single collective directed thought is all it takes to change the world."
~Lynne McTaggart

An interesting question; why do bad things happen to us all or to most people? I have often heard reports of people accusing God/Allah, etc. for allowing bad things to happen to them. Reports that such people couldn't come to terms with God for sitting there idly for worse things to come their way. Others going to the extreme of denying the existence of God or Supreme Intelligence or becoming so angry with God that if they had an opportunity to meet this guy, who calls himself God, they would just stab him repeatedly to death or something. I have been on that road before, where I once accused God of every single bad thing that I experienced in my life.

It is quite interesting the kind of accusations we level against God when things don't seem to work well for us. We often ask that, if God loves me why is my spouse dead or fallen sick, why have I lost my job? If God loves me why am I going through so much pain and rejection? If God loves me why this, why that, name the rest? It is intriguing to note that about 99.99% of the worse things we encounter in life hasn't got anything to do with the Grand God or even the devil. Well, this statement may be arguable to some point but in reality, God hasn't got any hand in the evil that we suffer in our lives.

> *"Hell, in my opinion, is never finding your true self and never living your own life or knowing who you are."*
> *~John Bradshaw*
> *Healing the Shame that Binds You*

At one time in my life, I used to think God had a hand in the evils I was experiencing. And at a point I was prepared to take God to court to answer for his alleged crimes against me and humanity; for allowing me to go through hell. It was funny though because I didn't know where and how I was going to summon this God to answer for his alleged crimes. I think God, whoever he or she is, one way or the other understood that I couldn't really take Him or Her to any court. What my soul was really interested in, was finding out why I was going through those challenges, what I had got to do with them, where they were from and how I was going to un-fuck myself from such hells.

Once I started asking the why, what and how questions, the universe furnished me with the necessary answers to those questions. And that resulted in my first book 'Create Your Own Life.' When life seemed really hard for me, I embarked on a journey of self-discovery. I had to know why I was going through those challenges. I had to know who was behind my sufferings. I was tired of the blame-game. I was tired of blaming the world systems. I was tired of blaming the government, my parents, etc. My mind wasn't going to take any more of the blame-games I was playing with myself. If fact, I blamed everybody but myself for all those negativities I was going through. Until I began to look deeper into myself, then I realized that the master brewer of my own sufferings was myself. I was the originator of my own woes. Once I discovered where all my sufferings were coming from, I knew exactly what to do. And you can discover the how for yourself via my book 'Create Your Own Life'.

"Within each of us is a light, awake, encoded in the fibers of our existence. Divine ecstasy is the totality of this marvelous creation experienced in the hearts of humanity."
~Tony Samara

It is often said that "to be human is to have stories to tell". Obviously, all of us humans have stories to tell; of our challenges and triumphs, of our pains and glories, of our lives and deaths, etc. The challenges we go through in life make us and unmake us. Some have suffered great tragedies and emerged stronger than before. Others suffered similar tragedies and that was the end of their lives. They lost all hopes in fighting forward with life. They just quitted on life and all that it had to offer them. Are you going to quit because you are going through something worse and you think you are the only one going through that?

No matter what is happening to your life, know that someone somewhere on planet Earth, is going through a lot more hell than you think you are going through. And you got only one option; to keep moving forward, to keep going, no matter what. Life is a force that needs to flow. Staying or being stagnant will only drain the life energy out of you; resulting in your slow demise. Don't be a living dead. Many people are alive physically but they are dead or slowing dying metaphysically or spiritually. They have lost their purpose and compass in life. They just don't know what to do with their lives. They are barely hanging on with their lives, waiting for something to come claim their lives. No matter what, don't join those group of people. Don't live your life like it hasn't got any meaning or purpose. No matter what happens, don't stagnant in life. Just keep moving.

Ok! Now let me attempt to answer why bad things happen to us, from the metaphysical (spirit-soul) and physical point of view. There may be a lot of reasons why bad things happen to us but for the purpose of this book, I would like to focus on such the two main reasons; reasons springing from the spirit-soul journey and the material (body, physical).

"Once all struggle is grasped, miracles are possible."
~Mao Zedong

The Spirit-Soul's Journey

"All of us are part of a beautiful pageantry of human experience. Let us make the most of this life in all we do."
~Laurence Overmire
A Revolutionary American Family: The McDonalds of Somerset County, New Jersey.

We are all on the journey of self-discovery. A journey to be; to become as God/Allah is. We are as God is from the metaphysical or spiritual point of view but upon becoming humans, we experience the divine in us all. The experiences we go through as spirit beings in flesh (humans), help us remember who we really are as gods. That's we evolve our spirits to this ultimate God-state through our physical and metaphysical experiences. Though we are all growing or evolving into this God-state, each individual spirit-soul's experience is unique to such spirit-soul.

We all choose our individual evolutionary paths as spirit beings even before we transit from the quantum/spiritual world to this material plane. As a result, our individual experiences are unique to ourselves. We may meet few individual spirit-souls such as families, friends, associates, etc. who may be vibrating on the same frequencies of life experiences whether good or bad, sharing similar fate with ourselves so that together we all evolve into the Godhead. Nevertheless, our experiences are unique to us. Our physical experiences are tied to what our spirit-souls set out to do in this incarnation. Our experiences are mostly influenced by our spirit-soul selves and these experiences in turn affect our spirit-soul state. Our bodies and spirit-souls are involved in an intricate enigmatic interchange of influences. The spirit-soul begets the body or the physical realm and the physical realm/body embellishes the spirit-soul via its experiences.

For example, an individual spirit-soul that is benign and rooted in love or the positive spectrum of spirituality, will result in the individual experiencing more of positive events in his or her life and these positive experiences then reinforce the state of the spirit-soul of the individual. Likewise, if a spirit-soul finds itself in the negative spectrum of spirituality, the resultant physical experiences will mostly be negatives; either the person suffers greatly at the hands of others or does great harm or evil to others or both, or worse. So, the path taken by the spirit-soul on its journey in the material plane does influence the good and bad that happen to us.

"We are the cosmos made conscious and life is the means by which the universe understands itself."
~Brian Cox

If the bad that happens to us sometimes originate from the spirit-soul, does that mean we can't change our fate? You may ask. I believe some happenstances to our lives; we are given the privy to change them or the outcome. Our fate is not sealed for good. There is some form of allowance accorded us to alter our destiny at will but as to how much alterations we can do to our destinies, I cannot tell. If the negatives happening to an individual on the material plane lie in the spirit-soul zone where we can change the outcome, then it is possible. There are other negatives that no matter how many times we try, the endpoint or possible outcome will always be the same. If the outcome of an event is fixed then it means that, that is what the spirit-soul of that individual has chosen to experience in its incarnation and nothing done in the material plane can change it.

While certain experiences we can't necessarily change the outcome, we can change how we feel about them. Changing how we feel about those negative experiences will give new meanings to these experiences. We will move from feeling and thinking bad about these experiences to where we embrace these experiences, and work them out or enjoy the process while it last, knowing very well that no amount of negativity can ultimately destroy us (the spirit-soul). The negative experiences can destroy the body alright. But we wouldn't be troubled knowing very well that we are not the body. That we are eternal spirit-souls that exist in and outside of this body and time.

Understand that it is not just your spirit-soul's journey into this material plane that affects our physical states and what happens to us. Like I said earlier on, our spirit-soul states affect our physicality and our physical states and experiences affect and enforce the state of our souls. Now that we have approached why bad things do happen to us, from the spirit-soul point of view, let's consider the other alternative; where our physical experiences contribute to the negativity we experience in our lives. Our perceptions and realities about life also contribute to what happens to us whether good or otherwise.

"The quality of our life is directly proportional to the quality of our thoughts."
~Avijeet Das.

Perception

The Observer Effect

In a study reported in Nature (Vol. 391, pp. 871-874), researchers at the Weizmann Institute of Science conducted a highly controlled experiment that demonstrated how a beam of electrons is affected by the sheer act of being observed. The experiment showed that the greater the amount of "watching," the higher the observer's influence or effect on what actually takes place. This phenomenon is what has become commonly referred to as the observer effect. It is a known fact in quantum mechanics that the observer (researcher/ detector) trying to determine the end results of an experiment influences the end results.

'Nature' is a highly prestigious peer-reviewed scientific journal. All experiments or research works submitted to this

journal for publication go through the process of assessment, scrutiny and consideration from expert researchers in related fields before they get published.

[1]To demonstrate that this observer effect wasn't only limited to particle physics or quantum mechanics, different independent researchers decided to test this theory or hypothesis using human DNA strand. In the experiment, a DNA strand was introduced into a chamber filled with light photons or particles. In the absence of the DNA strand, the light photons behaved randomly. There was no form or structure to the photons. When the DNA was introduced into this chamber, the photons began to rearrange themselves to form the double helix structure of the DNA. That is, the light photons began to take on the shape and likeness of the DNA. The DNA in some way induced some electromagnetic influence on the photons to cause them to take on its shape and structure. This really intrigued the scientists. The study was repeated by another group of researchers and they came to the same conclusion like the initial researchers. That DNA strand do have some form of effect on its environment.

What this meant was that we are not just beings going through life anyway, anyhow. Our intentions expressed as information or energy in our genes or DNA have the capacity to influence the physical world. Whether knowingly or unknowingly, positive or negative, whatever we are made of internally, gets expressed outwards into the physical world. We influence our physical world or space energetically. It became clear to these scientists that observer effect wasn't something that was only limited to particles at the quantum level but protein synthesis or biological component like the DNA could somewhat affect its environment and what it interacts with.

> *"Perception is more important than reality. If someone perceives something to be true, it is more important than if it is in fact true. This doesn't mean you should be duplicitous or deceitful, but don't go out of your way to correct a false assumption if it plays to your advantage."*
> *~Ivanka Trump*
> *The Trump Card: Playing to Win in Work and Life.*

On a micro or cellular scale, the effect of DNA strand on its environs, may not be hugely felt or expressed. But on a macro scale like the full human body, the expression of our genes or the manifestation of information in our genes to the physical plane is profound when observed carefully. [2]The human body is known to contain about 20,000 to 25,000 genes, according to U.S. National Library of Medicine. All these numerous genes contain DNA strands. So just imagine the collective expression of the genes in our body.

[3]For several years, scientists thought that our gene expressions were set from birth. Nothing else influenced our gene expressions. That is, whatever information we inherited from our parents were set and ruled our lives. But a new branch of science, epigenetics, suggests otherwise. Without being too

technical, epigenetics is the study of how our environment and lifestyle affect our gene expressions and how these gene expressions reinforce or validate our lifestyles and environments. It is like our genes, environments and lifestyles are in constant information sharing loop via some quantum entanglement processes where whatever happens to one affects the others whether good or otherwise.

According to epigenetics, if our lifestyles (belief systems, thoughts, actions, diet, etc.) do influence and affect our gene expressions and the DNA in our genes can affect matter (the physical world), then it means that our perceptions (thoughts, ideologies, belief systems, etc.) can and do affect the physical plane. Our thoughts, words and actions do become flesh in the physical plane. We literally manifest whatever we hold true in our minds. This is where we incarnate and exhibit the power of the gods; our minds, to create whatever outcome for our lives, whether good or otherwise. The pains and struggles that happen in life, are all by our creation. Our perceptions or thoughts affect the internal state of our bodies. Our internal worlds get manifested in the physical plane. The occurrences in the physical world then confirm and re-enforce our perceptions of reality; what we hold or believe to be real about life.

> *"The world we see and experience is actually our personal interpretation of vibrational waves."*
> *~Melissa Heisler*
> *From Type A to Type Me: How to Stop "Doing" Life and Start Living It*

Consider this example, a girl thinks and accepts that all men are liars and cheaters. A girl's body accepts this perception as the truth and expresses it out there. This expressed reality goes out in the form of energy waves to search for its equivalence and finds a man that fits such description. A man comes a girl's way to cheat and lie to her. So that her reality of who men are becomes confirmed and validated. A girl gets brokenhearted, thinks and believes that all men are the same. And as long as she thinks all men are the same, she experiences the same men, to validate her perceptions that all men are the same. And this goes on and on onto infinity.

This is just one example. Almost every bad thing that happens to us has its root cause in our thoughts, feelings and how we perceive the world. To the person who thinks and feels that life is a struggle, life has no option than to present struggles to this individual in order to agree to his or her truth about what life is. To such individuals, every facet of their lives is full of struggles. Likewise, to the individual who thinks and sees the positivity of life. He or she enjoys the blissfulness of life thereof. So, whatever we think and perceive to be true about our lives becomes our truth and this truth materialize in the physical world, whether good or otherwise. These things influence our perception of life and reality; our belief systems, feelings, thoughts, words and actions. These maintain a closed cycle of interactions and influence one another, and this collectively influences how we see the world and life. Our perceptions of who we are and how we see the world influence the happenstances of our lives whether good or otherwise.

How does the observer effect changes in that which is being observed? It's very simple. Everything in this universe including ourselves is made of energy, and energy interacts with itself. We are just energy incarnated in flesh; which is also energy vibrating at a very slow rate. Our thoughts, words, actions, feelings are all different forms of energy that have the power to influence other forms of energies around us. Just that these energetic interactions can be somewhat subtle to the point that we hardly feel the effect thereof. Our internal energies in the form of thoughts, emotions and belief systems influence our external worlds and how our lives unfold.

"All that we see or seem is but a dream within a dream."
~Edgar Allan Poe

Belief Systems: The Silent Lords That Run Our Lives

"Reality is a construct of the neurons."
~Abhijit Naskar , What is Mind?

What do you believe in, about yourself and life? How do you see yourself? How do you see life to be? Are these beliefs of yourself and life really true? Or these beliefs appear to be true because you believe them and want them to be true? Are your beliefs about yourself and life actually your own beliefs or something you somewhat inherited or learned from your family, society, environment, etc.? Do you own your belief systems? A greater percentage of what we believe to be true about who we are and what life is all about isn't our own generated beliefs but something that was transferred to us through our genes and also through our interactions with the environment where we grew up.

And did you know that about 95% of our lives is ran by these belief systems that have become so buried deeply within our subconscious mind? From the neurological point of view, our wakeful conscious mind/brain only accounts for just 5% of our lives. Just 5%. The 95% of who we are and become in life is governed by our subconscious mind, where all our beliefs and unexpressed emotions are buried. And these run our lives unknowingly. Many of us don't know that all our struggles about life do come from thoughts or beliefs that are deeply rooted in our subconscious mind. If only we could reach deep into ourselves and alter the mind programs passed onto us from childhood, we could change our lives for the better.

> *"The world is full of magic things, patiently waiting for our senses to grow sharper."*
> *~W.B. Yeats*

Let me explain further by borrowing from computer science-engineering perspective. When Dell or any other computer manufacturing brand builds a new computer; whether desktop or laptop, it comes out from the assembly-line blank; with no software running it. Then depending on the preference of the market, an operating system software is installed. Operating Software/System can be Windows OS, Mac OS, Linux OS, Android OS, etc. Once an operating system/software is installed, the operating software becomes the governing system of the computer.

That's to say, every other software installed after the installation of the operating software, should have similar coding with the operating software, in order to interact effectively with the operating software on the computer. The buyer or manufacturer of the computer cannot install software built for Mac OS on Windows OS or Linux OS. It simply won't work out unless the buyer or manufacturer changes the operating software.

The human being or body functions more or less like a computer. We are what I prefer to call 'organic or biological computers'. A newly born baby can be compared to a newly built computer. It comes empty-headed, with absolutely nothing on its hard drive (mind). The baby born into a family, society, community, country, etc. gets programmed effectively and accordingly as it grows.

> *"Believe that life is worth living and your belief will help create the fact."*
> *~ William James.*

The brain or mind of the baby becomes programmed by the values and limitations of its immediate environments; family, school, church or mosque, society, etc., from day 1 to about 7 years old. Neurologists stipulate that, after age 7 of a child, the rest of his or her life becomes repetition of whatever transpired and got recorded in his or her subconscious mind from age 0 to 7. This means the operating system/software of the child's life becomes installed from age 0 to 7, whether good or otherwise.

Any life experiences of this child after age 7 are mostly in line with what got installed on its biological hard drive: the subconscious mind. Any software installed on a computer after the installation of the operating software/system must agree to the coding of the particular OS, in order for the whole computer to work harmoniously. The same is true when it comes to this biological computer system; humans. Any life experiences that get installed in the subconscious mind, particularly from the ages of 0 to 7, run our lives. The conscious mind perceives and accepts them to be true. This acceptance then enforces and reinforces the activities of the subconscious mind, in order to generate more of that which was accepted as truth. Then the cycle continues from childhood till adulthood and death.

"Humans see what they want to see."
~Rick Riordan
The Lightning Thief (Percy Jackson and the Olympians, #1)

Let's consider this scenario, a girl child observes her mother experience abusive treatment from the father. The girl grows into adulthood and finds herself in an abusive relationship and she doesn't understand why she is suffering the same fate as the mother some years back. What happened in her childhood formed part of what she believed to be true about the relationship between lovers, subconsciously. A girl then becomes confused because consciously she desires relationships with happy endings but subconsciously, her programming is about experiencing abusive relationship as the best or only option.

As long as her programming or subconscious mind says it wants abusive relationship, the girl will jump from one abusive relationship to another, until that deep-rooted message about relationship be cleared from her subconscious mind. Remember, the subconscious mind can't tell the difference between good and bad. It just accepts things as they are. It is the conscious analytical mind that differentiate between good and bad, and that analytical mind comes into dominant use after age 7, according to neurological studies.

Can we undo the family and societal programs of the subconscious mind? Yes! We can delete any unwanted programs that have formed part or become our belief system, and reprogram our subconscious mind, just like we can uninstall computer operating system/software and install new ones. There are a lot of techniques out there both medically and metaphysically speaking. Medically speaking, one can use hypnotic therapies to reverse engineer the subconscious mind. Spiritually or metaphysically speaking, one can also change the state of the subconscious mind via prayers, meditations, yoga, etc.

What of positive affirmation? You may be wondering. Affirmations alone may take forever to work or not work at all. This is because you are using the conscious mind, which is just 5% to change something in the subconscious mind, which accounts for 95% of your being. A lot of effort and energy will be expended to do that. What works best for me and what will work best for you especially if you are not interested in hypnotic therapies, is to combine the positive affirmations with meditation.

"Quiet the mind, and the soul will speak."
~Ma Jaya Sati Bhagavati

Meditation when properly done, can help your mind to relax thereby moving your brain waves from the alpha state (*the conscious mind operates in this wave form; alpha state*) to the theta state (*the brainwave at which the subconscious mind operates or is accessible*). At this theta brainwave state, whatever you implant or suggest to your mind bypasses the conscious analytical barrier of the mind and moves directly into the subconscious mind. Consistent meditation coupled with positive affirmations can reverse engineer any negative programs in the subconscious mind, to make way for the new positive ones.

I've tried this meditation coupled with positive affirmations and it works very fine and fast as well. I've manifested money, travels, jobs, etc. with this approach and it works great. All I ever do is get myself into meditative state to relax and transition my brainwave from the alpha to theta state where I can readily have access to the power of my subconscious mind. Then in that meditative state, I suggest an image or idea of what I want manifested in the physical plane. I feel the feeling of having received that which I want manifested and depending on when I desire those things to be manifested, everything appears physically as seen or programmed into my subconscious mind, in that meditative state.

"Remember that what you believe will depend very much on what you are."
~ Noah Porter

Possibly in a near future I will write a book on the whole process detailing everything but for the purpose of this book, let's keep it brief, simple and straight forward. [4]Meditation has about 72 scientifically backed or documented benefits. It reduces stress hormone level in the body. You can heal yourself via meditation and I have done that before. And this operates on the same principle. Go into a meditative state to access the power of your subconscious mind. Suggest to the subconscious mind that you are healed and whole. Come out of the meditative state. Allow the subconscious mind to do the rest. And many more benefits that I can't list them all here. Don't use this meditation suggestion to replace medical care. Seek medical attention if your illness dictates so. This meditative approach may not work especially if there are other blockades in your subconscious mind that need to be removed before effective healing can take place and you don't know of or have any clue of what they are.

"Meditation is realizing and expanding your inner beauty in every direction."
~Amit Ray

Emotions/Feelings: The Mistress at the House of Lords

"Man often becomes what he believes himself to be. If I keep on saying to myself that I cannot do a certain thing, it is possible I may end by really becoming incapable of doing it. On the contrary, if I shall have the belief that I can do it, I shall surely acquire the capacity to do it, even if I may not have it at the beginning."
~ Mahatma Gandhi.

If belief systems with its relatives are the silent lords of our lives, then their partner is the emotions or feelings we attach to these belief systems. The two are inseparable; our emotions and belief systems. The reason we are able to remember events that happened to us in our childhood stages, whether good or otherwise, is because of the emotions we associate or associated with them. Even our whole life makes meaning to us, not just because of our beliefs but also because of the associated emotions.

Let's use this scenario as an example of why I am alleging that emotions somewhat add meaning to our life experiences. Let's say you meet someone in the train or car, you strike a conversation. You get his or her contact before you depart to your separate destinations. You continue your conversation later on and fall in love with each other. You become fond of each other and gain each other's attention. All of a sudden you like the dress code and hairstyle or haircut of a person you just met. You become so engrossed with each other. Let's say you attend a function without your partner and you see someone wearing similar dress and haircut/style, you instantly become reminded of your lover. And you feel warmth towards that person and your lover as well.

"Your emotions are the slaves to your thoughts, and you are the slave to your emotions."
~ Elizabeth Gilbert

Now let's assume for some reason, the relationship between you and your partner ends bitterly, the very same dress or hairstyle or haircut that gave you some form of warm feeling when you saw it on others, will likely make you loathe or angry, after the breakup. Though the same dress but the emotions associated with it has changed from being that of love to that of hatred and jealousy. In a matter of moments, you have moved from love to hatred and nothing has really changed about the dress or haircut. You have changed. You have given meaning to the event because of the emotions you have associated with it.

Life with its experiences normally come without any meanings to it. They are just what they are; energies in motions or experiential moments in space-time continuum. But what we make of these experiences are entirely up to us and the emotions that we associate with them. These emotions coupled with our beliefs help create meaning out of all our life experiences. Our beliefs and emotions are all subjective. Because these two are subjective and personalized, we interpret the world around us through this skewed perception, leading to our different life experiences.

If you really want to know the origins of your woes and how to fix them, look to your beliefs or belief systems and most importantly the emotions associated with these systems or thoughts. Jesus Christ said in the Gospel of Thomas verse 22 that "when you make the two one… then will you enter the kingdom." What this means is that, when we learn to make the mind (thoughts, belief systems) and the heart (emotions) one, then you can create whatever life experience we want or desire, whether good or otherwise. These are the most two powerful creative forces or units in our bodies; the mind (thoughts) and the heart (emotions). Whenever these two are in agreement with each other, we can manifest whatever we desire from the spiritual world to the physical plane, with time. In reverse, if things aren't going well for you, it means it is either the two (heart and mind) are not in agreement with each other or the agreement between these two units are in the negative spectrum of life experiences.

> *"One ought to hold on to one's heart; for if one lets it go,*
> *one soon loses control of the head too."*
> *~ Friedrich Nietzsche.*

There Is Good In The Bad

The Absolute World vs. the Relative World

"People will do anything, no matter how absurd, in order to avoid facing their own souls. One does not become enlightened by imagining figures of light, but by making the darkness conscious."
~Carl Jung
Psychology and Alchemy (Collected Works 12)

Another classic reason why bad things do happen and sometimes to us, is that we live in a relative world. What do I mean by 'relative world'? In a relative world, two particles of opposite charges coexist in the same system to create a balanced world. That is, one particle cannot exist if its opposite-charged neighbor isn't available. Then we have what I call the absolute world. In an absolute world, one particle can exist perfectly and harmoniously without its opposite pair. In an absolute realm of existence, a positive particle can exist alone without any interactions with its negative pair. Theoretically speaking, in the realms of physics, relative worlds do exist, where everything measured is in relation to something else, either a background microwave energy or anything. I don't know if there are absolute worlds as well; where particles exist without any relation to or with their opposite pairs and other particles.

We live in a relative world, where good cannot exist without bad. Simple logic dictates that if only good were to exist in our material world, we wouldn't be able to tell the difference between that which is good and that which is bad. So, when we look around us, almost everything that exists in nature exist in pairs. We have light and darkness, male and female, good and bad, life and death, love and hatred, etc. Both pairs are needed for us to make sense of ourselves and environments. Bad things have their place in our co-creative experiences, though that shouldn't have been the case with our evolutionary path. We as a race have collectively selected, created or chosen our evolutionary path where negative events are featured. So that out of the negativity, we will remember who we are as gods and the power that we wield to change our fates.

"Peace, happiness, and love are a daily practice. Give time and energy to that which you want more of in your life. Invest in yourself for a higher quality of life. You're worth it."
~Akiroq Brost

Understand that nothing really happens to us without the involvement of our will. To the person who gets murdered, it is in his or her eternal will that at certain point in his or her journey on Earth, he or she should be murdered. I know you are wondering why it should be in the eternal will of someone for him or her to be murdered. But think of it this way, how will one experience himself or herself as a murderer if there's no one to be murdered? Remember in the beginning of the book I said that all there is to life is experiences. Life is experiential moments in space-time where we all experience the good and bad in ourselves. Does that mean the murderer shouldn't be brought to justice?

Of course, the murderer should be imprisoned or punished for killing and I'm not saying also that we should go about, doing evil to others if it's in our capacity to do good to them. What I'm implying is that we are all experiencing who we are, and some chose their life experiences from the negative spectrum of events. The thing is, how could even God exhibit his or her saving grace and forgiveness if Adam and Eve didn't f*ck up in the Garden of Eden? For God to show his or her forgiveness, healing, etc. towards us, somebody had to f*ck him or her up and luckily enough it was Adam and Eve. So, there's some form of good in the bad that sometimes happens to us all.

"If your mind carries a heavy burden of past, you will experience more of the same. The past perpetuates itself through lack of presence. The quality of your consciousness at this moment is what shapes the future."
~Eckhart Tolle
The Power of Now: A Guide to Spiritual Enlightenment.

Bad things operate within certain frequencies and as long as we collectively think and act within those particular frequencies, bad things will keep coming our ways as individuals and as collective consciousness. We will keep experiencing bad things as long as we maintain our spirit-soul vibrations within the frequency range of negativity. But there's a way out. If only we can raise our spiritual energies or vibrations above that of the frequencies of negativity, we will experience shift in our collective conscious experiences. The bad will fade into the background and in its place, the good will flourish.

It isn't about raising our awareness of evil say breast cancer and the likes. It's about raising our awareness above these negative happenstances. Raising our awareness of evil only intensifies the evil, because now our whole collective focus dwells on the negativity and as long as we focus on the negatives, we give life to them. They grow and blossom over time. But when we raise our focus, awareness or consciousness above these negative elements, then with time these elements become starved and die out of existence.

"Create daily habits that will create a higher quality of life. Remember, our lives become whatever we practice."
~Akiroq Brost

Raising our awareness, consciousness or spiritual energies above these elemental demons or negativities, can come about in many different ways. Via meditation, yogi, prayers, etc., we can increase our spiritual energies above these elemental negativities. Find out what works best for you. If yours is to call on the name of Jesus Christ, then do it wholeheartedly without criticizing or condemning the one who doesn't call on the name of Jesus Christ. If yours is to go to the mosque and pray, then do it. Whatever appeals to your faith, which will help you to be more spiritually conscious or inclined, do it?

In effect, we are all after the same goal: to be more spiritually inclined or to raise our spiritual energies/awareness. Though individually our paths may be different but collectively we are all heading towards the same destination with our lives; to grow into the Godhead or to be as God/Allah is, to re-member who we are as gods (become reconnected to our Source).

"We are consciousness incarnated in stardust..."
~Graham Hancock

If we can raise our collective consciousness vibrations, then we will be ushered into the absolute realm of existence, a realm where evil necessarily doesn't exist but all there is, is good. I think this is what many Christians and religious philosophies call 'heaven'. And in this realm of the absolute, we don't need the presence of evil for us to know that which is good. We will have so much power in our being that we can literally time travel into our past just to infer from the negativities of our past lives. Moreover, by quantum entanglement, we can maintain inferences from our evil pasts without necessarily dwelling together with them like in our present state of being. By so doing, we will maintain the cosmic balance without necessarily dwelling together with evil, like in our present state of being. Let's talk more about this in part 3 of the book under the topic 'all things are working together for your becoming.

"The power of an intention multiplies, depending upon how many people are thinking the same thought at the same time."
~Lynne McTaggart

References

1. DNA effect on light photons: https://medium.com/@igorgurko/three-experiments-that-change-everything-2bc578480d34). Date accessed: December 2019.
2. The Human Genome Project: https://ghr.nlm.gov/primer/hgp/description Date accessed: January 2020.
3. Epigenetics and the environment: https://www.google.com/amp/s/www.irunfar.com/2013/10/epigenetics-how-our-lifestyle-can-impact-our-genes.html. Date accessed: January 2020.
4. Benefits of Meditation: https://liveanddare.com/benefits-of-meditation. Date accessed: July 2019.

PART 3

Intentionally left blank

The Tree of Life

Why It Should Be You and Not Someone Else

"...whatsoever a man soweth, that shall he also reap."
~Galatians 6:7 KJV

Most of us if not all, are familiar with the biblical story of Adam and Eve, the tree of knowledge of good and evil, and the tree of life. We know a lot of the tree of knowledge of good and evil but very little is known about the tree of life. Per the biblical account, Adam and Eve were sacked from the Garden of Eden after tampering with the tree of knowledge of good and evil. Let me borrow this concept from the biblical account to illustrate why it should be you and not someone else, to go through what you are going through whether good or otherwise.

I know in part 2, we looked at why bad things happen to us from the spiritual/metaphysical and perceptional points of view. So, I am not going to repeat them again. In this part, we are going to look at the tree of life and how it pertains to you and your life experiences. Where tree of life in this context doesn't necessarily mean or represent that Tree of Life in the Garden of Eden but using a tree as an illustration of life and its experiences.

"Turn your wounds into wisdom."
~ Oprah Winfrey

Before we go ahead to study the tree of life, let's first consider that which gives birth to the tree: the seed(s). What are the seeds of life? The seeds can be the thoughts, ideas and words about life that we hear from our parents, friends, siblings, school, etc., during childhood stage. The seeds can also be our own thoughts and ideologies about life; the personalized definitions that we give to life even as we grow and move through the process of becoming. The soil: the subconscious mind of a child which doesn't filter the good from the bad, serves as a fertile ground for these seeds to germinate and grow. Life experiences of a child's immediate family members and other grown-ups can also serve as seeds for the child's subconscious mind.

We learnt from part 2 that from age zero to seven of a child is the crucial moments in his or her mental and hence life development. The conscious analytical mind, which is able to differentiate between good and otherwise, is under-developed between these age ranges, according to neuroscience. Every thoughts, ideas, words and actions of the guardian, fed to a child between these years of his or her development, gets processed and accepted by the subconscious mind as true or real. These seeds grow and form the bases of the child's understanding of what life is.

Evidence from neuroscience suggests that whatever happens after age 7 of a child's life is just repetition of what transpired between age 0 and 7. The seeds sown between these ages of 0 and 7 become the foundation or the roots of the tree of life of that child, whether what were sown were good or otherwise. The roots grow deeper into the subconscious mind and outward to form the trunk, branches, leaves and fruits in the course of the development of the child into adulthood. In a typical tree development, the roots give the tree an anchorage, support and nourishment from the soil.

In the life of a human being, the roots of the tree of life become the beliefs, belief systems about life and the personalized meaning thereof. These systems serve as an anchorage and provide nourishment from the subconscious mind to the individual's life. Without these roots, the individual and his or her conscious mind cannot make any meaning out of life. The roots of this tree of life of an individual depends largely on the kind of seeds sown, whether positive or negative. And the kind of seeds sown also depends on the background of that individual; where he or she grew up.

"Life is like riding a bicycle. To keep your balance, you must keep moving."
~ Albert Eisntein

Now that we understand what the roots of this tree of life mean, let's consider another part of the tree; the trunk. The trunk of a tree serves as a link between the roots and the leaves. Food or energies produced by the leaves are transferred through the trunk to the roots. Minerals and nutrients in the soil are picked by the roots and transferred through the trunk or stem to the leaves. The conscious mind represents the trunk of the tree of life. Our conscious mind serves as a link between that which is buried within our subconscious mind and that which manifests in our lives as experiences. Our life experiences likewise get processed by the conscious mind and added to the existing programs of the subconscious mind. These life experiences reinforce the existing programs of the subconscious mind.

"As you sow in your subconscious mind, so shall you reap in your body and environment."
~ Joseph Murphy, The Power of the Subconscious Mind

Scientifically speaking, 95% of our lives are governed by our subconscious mind and the programs thereof. Only about 5% of our minds is conscious. This part of our mind often serves as a temporary storage system for our life experiences, just as a tree trunk can store food, energies or information from its internal and external experiences. In a nutshell, our conscious mind; the part of us which makes it possible for us to be aware of who we claim to be, and our environments, serves as a central point; a point between our subconscious mind and our life experiences.

[1]For example, when an individual starts to learn a new skill, he or she starts off with the conscious mind. It is slow, tasking and demand a lot of mental power to learn something new. But the more this individual keeps at it, the less demanding the new skill becomes. Over time, this individual then masters the skill and can deliver without necessarily thinking about it. With time, this new acquired skill becomes like an automated system to the brain or mind. The reason is that after he or she starts off with the conscious mind, the more he or she progresses with the new skill acquisition, the less it gets to involve the conscious mind. The conscious part of our brain is very slow in processing data as compared to the subconscious part of the brain. Whiles the conscious part can process a few thousand data per time, the subconscious part can process data in millions per time. This makes the subconscious mind a reservoir of knowledge and experiences. And with the conscious mind, we add up to this reservoir of experiences and also draw from the memory of the subconscious mind.

"Watch your thoughts; they become words. Watch your words; they become actions. Watch your actions; they become habits. Watch your habits; they become character. Watch your character; it becomes your destiny."
~ Lao-Tze

Moving upwards from the trunk of the tree of life, we go to the branches and leaves of the tree. The branches and leaves represent our knowledge and actions respectively. The branches are in closed circuit or relation with the leaves and the trunk of the tree. The branches receive of the leaves as well as the trunk of the tree. That is, the knowledge of who we are and what the world is, is in close association with the actions we take and the information we already have in our subconscious/conscious mind.

The trunk, represented as the conscious mind, can have different branches. The branches become those compartmentalized areas of the conscious mind. Each compartmentalized section represents the different views, knowledge or perceptions of who we are and what life means to us. These sections influence and affect the necessary actions we take towards ourselves, others and life as a whole. Our actions coupled with external stimuli result in our life experiences aka the fruits of the tree of life.

A lot of things go into the production of fruits by a typical fruit-bearing tree like mango or orange tree: nutrients in the soil, sorption capacity of the tree's root for nutrients and water from the soil, the tree's trunk capacity to relay the nutrients and water from the roots to the branches and the leaves, ability of the leaves to receive sunlight and carbon dioxide for photosynthesis, etc. The fruits of the tree of life aka our life experiences follow similar path in their making. All our life experiences are outward manifestations of our inner worlds. They embody all that we hold true in our being, whether good or otherwise and whether consciously or unconsciously. Our personalized definitions of life coupled with our internal construction of how life should be, give rise to our outward experiences about life, whether good or otherwise.

"You have brains in your head. You have feet in your shoes. You can steer yourself any direction you choose."
~ Dr. Seuss

For example, when an individual, holds in his or her being that he or she isn't enough, nothing in such an individual's life will be enough. Everything will have the 'not-enough' tag on it. From personal experiences, jobs, marriage or relationships, children, etc., everything will have that 'not-enough' tag. The end result will be that such an individual will live in a hyper state of 'not-enough-ness' where there's anxiety, fear, ungratefulness, etc. This then leads to poor health which reinforces his or her perception of 'not-enough' health. Interestingly when we eat of the tree of life or go through the experiences we help create; they serve as seeds that get sown into our subconscious minds. These seeds serve as nourishment to the ones already existing in our minds. The more of the experiences we have, the more the minds want to experience and the bigger the tree of life becomes.

Understand that when your life experiences aren't going well as you desire them to go, the outside world has very little to do with it. Just like the sunlight and carbon dioxide of the atmosphere do not determine what kind of fruit a tree should bear, likewise your external environments. Your boss isn't the reason why you are not happy in the workplace. The economy hasn't got anything to do with why you may be poor or broke. In the same 'hard economy', someone is super rich. Stop blaming all your bad experiences on the outside stimuli. These outside stimuli only respond to what is happening inside of you. The sunlight stimulates the leaves of a plant to bear fruits according to its kind. It doesn't dictate to the plant what kind of fruits to bear.

"Life is what we make it, always has been, always will be"
~ Grandma Moses

To understand why you, and why you have certain repeated and unpleasant experiences in many different forms, search yourself. Go deeper into yourself. What are your deepest fears and woes? What are your grey areas: areas you prefer not to approach or talk about and make up every possible excuse to avoid them altogether? What did you suffer as a child? Do these childhood sufferings continue to show up in your life in different forms? Are you reliving your past experiences but in different forms? Your dad left your mum when you were a child and you became so angry with your dad and never forgave him for leaving you and your mum. You grew up as an adult and every man that comes your way as a lover ends up leaving, no matter what, just like your dad left your mum. This isn't a coincidence or the devil trying to ruin your life.

You are reliving your childhood experiences and as long as you have the bitterness energy against your dad in you, you will keep experiencing the same thing over and over again. You need to let go and be free of your past. In effect, nothing really matters and every experience is another moment in the eternal moment of Now. All our emotions are meant to pass through us, not for us to hold onto them, because they are energies in motion. Hence the term 'e-motions'. They are not meant to stay forever inside of us. They are meant to pass through us and continue to the 'no-thingness'. That's why we have memory. When we remember an experience, we reconnect our consciousness or awareness to that experience stored in the 'no-thingness', which then brings back all the associated emotions through some weird quantum processes.

"Too many of us are not living our dreams because we are living our fears."
~ Les Brown

Be Responsible

"Your time is limited, do don't waste it living someone else's life. Don't be trapped by dogma – which is living with the results of other people's thinking."
~ *Steve Jobs*

In the previous chapter, I did talk about not blaming anyone outside of ourselves for the things that happen to us. Needless to say, don't blame yourself either for the things that come your way. But rather, be responsible or assume responsibility for the things that do happen to you. Everything that comes your way, whether good or otherwise, you have a part to play in its occurrence, whether consciously or unconsciously. Nothing really happens to you that's outside your will or doing. Everything is intricately interconnected and upon careful analysis of your woes, you will notice that everything will lead back to you. You are the source or originator of almost everything that happens to you. That's, you orchestrate your happenstances either spiritually or physically or both. Not the devil, not even God/Allah. You did and you still do.

"When I was 5 years old, my mother always told me that happiness was the key to life. When I went to school, they asked me what I wanted to be when I grew up. I wrote down 'happy'. They told me I didn't understand the assignment, and I told them they didn't understand life."
~ John Lennon

Metaphysically or spiritually speaking, you chose the kind of beings you will identify yourself with as your parents, when you transit the physical world even before you were born. You mapped out all your experiences, from birth to death; all your sufferings and glorious moments. I know how crazy this idea is but in effect that's exactly what happened to all of us before transiting into this physical world. At this moment, your spirit-soul knows exactly when its evolutionary journey as this you will come to an end in this world. It knows exactly what will happen for it to leave this body of yours and transit into the spiritual plane. It knows what kind of beings will transit through you to this world as your children. It knows of all the other you spread across the multi universe, living slightly different and independent lives yet connected to you and your life here on Earth.

Multi universe popularly known as multiverse is a concept in science that suggests that there are infinite or multiple universes just like ours out there with infinite number of earths with multiple versions of ourselves living slightly different lifestyles. This multiverse hypothesis originated from some findings in string theory physics and other physics disciplines. While this multiverse hypothesis hasn't been proven yet, I've had dream state experiences that suggest the existence of worlds or earths similar to ours with different versions of ourselves living slightly different lifestyles. I've had lucid dreams where I have interacted with familiar people in a slightly different way than I do interact with in my wakeful life. I've met different versions of people I know in my wakeful reality, in my dreams. I've seen different versions of myself; versions of me that don't fit into my past or future self. Those versions were me but kind of different me. All in my dreams. And it's only a matter of time before science catches up to these alternate realities.

I am not asking you or anyone to compulsorily believe in or reject this whole multiverse something. After all there's a lot to the human spirit-soul and the universe that we don't know.

"Don't limit yourself. Many people limit themselves to what they think they can do. You can go as far as your mind lets you. What you believe, remember, you can achieve."
~ Mary Kay Ash

For you to enjoy the best out of your life, you have to be responsible for your own life and the outcomes thereof whether good or otherwise. This is because knowing very well that everything that happens to you, happens according to your own will or desires and wishes whether good or otherwise, can help liberate and give you the agility required to navigate life challenges. Even if you were born with deformed body, you will understand and appreciate it that you chose that path for the evolution of your spirit-soul and you chose it for a purpose. That there's nothing for you to be ashamed of, about who you are. We live in a world where our structured school and parental system do not teach us to be responsible for our lives and the outcomes thereof. And this is doing the world a great disservice. Most parents spoon-feed and shield their wards from the harsh conditions of the world in the name of protection. Our schools do likewise by providing a safe environment for studies, cutting us off from what is happening in the real world.

It's interesting that these days we don't go to school to gain knowledge and skills. We go to get a job. We gain the knowledge alright but the motivation for gaining the knowledge for most of Earth's inhabitants is to secure a job afterwards. After leaving school, we expect someone, a company or the government to employ us. After employment, we expect our employers to take care of us and our children till we retire or die along the way. We expect medical care from our employers among other benefits, not just for ourselves but also for our children, as if the children are the employer's. And when we don't get jobs to do, we blame it on the government, as if it were the government who gave birth to us. No wonder our world's governmental structure is so manipulative and demeaning because that's what happens when we handover responsibility of our lives to the government and to our employers.

"You must expect great things of yourself before you can do them."
~ Michael Jordon

There should be systems to support earth's inhabitants. That I agree but it shouldn't also be the case where we depend solely and entirely on these systems for our lives and what we become. The systems should be there to support and not to sustain us. As long as we keep raising children through our homes and schools, who grow old to think that their parents, society and nation as a whole owes them for being children and citizens respectively, the systems will keep getting more and more choked until everything comes crumbling down. And everything will come crumbling down one day.

As individuals we should be responsible for our lives and actions. We should own up to the outcomes of our lives whether good or otherwise. Your life is your life. It isn't your mother's or father's. It isn't your government's. It is your life. Yes, your mother and father gave birth to you, you live in a country and pay tax. Nevertheless, your life is yours and you should be the one in charge. You should be the one responsible for what you become, not your parents or the society. If you are a teenager, young adult reading this, don't rely too much on your parents to take care of you. What will you do if your parents should die before you become an adult or something? Will you survive on your own or with little or no help from your extended family members or you will blame God for taking your mother and father away from you?

> *"The best way to predict your future is to create it."*
> *~ Abraham Lincoln*

Go out there, make mistakes, learn and grow. Go out there, start a business, fail at it, lose money, cry over your loss, learn and grow. Almost every person who made it to the top never relied too much on their parents, teachers or the government. They learnt to leverage these support systems and they never truly relied on them. Parents! Stop shielding your children from the harsh realities of the world. Instead, usher them gradually into it. Teach them to take initiatives and actions on their own. Teach them to risk and fail because in effect nothing really matters. All that matters is the evolution of our individual spirit-souls into the Godhead or God-state.

It doesn't matter how many mistakes we make, how many lifetimes we embody, we will eventually grow into this Godhead or state. It doesn't matter whether we die today or tomorrow, because we can't escape it. We will eventually die. So why not forget about death, and live life to the best of your knowledge and abilities. Live! Live! Live! Because no matter what you do, you will surely die one day. There's no escape from death. At least not in the near future. Probably in some thousands of years to come, we would advance to the point that we will become immortal. But for now, we will all surely die one day so don't let that deter you from living. Live but in your living, assume responsibility for your life and the outcomes thereof.

> *"It is our choices that show what we truly are, far more than our abilities."*
> ~ *J. K. Rowling*

Don't blame your failures on the government. Don't blame your struggles on the system, your employer, parents, siblings or anyone else. None of these entities are responsible for who and what has become of you. Your dad left you and so what? Your dad didn't take care of you, and so what? Is your life yours or your dad's or mum's? So why blame them for your actions and inactions. I've heard and read of individuals who become homeless after they lost their jobs and house. They lived and slept on the streets. But once these individuals had enough of blaming the system for their woes and assumed responsibility for their very lives, some moved from sleeping on the streets to building multi-million-dollar companies. Once these individuals realized they were there not because of the government, their employer or some bankers they owed, but by their own actions and inactions, they were able to transform their situation. They moved from homelessness to becoming CEOs of their own establishments.

There's no personal growth and maturity in blaming everything and everyone but ourselves for our failures and woes. Real growth and maturity lie in us assuming responsibility for who we become; our actions and inactions alike. Quit blaming the devil or God because none of these entities have anything to do with your troubles. You are going through the difficulties and not doing anything about it, because you kind of like it. You just like to complain, chime and whine about them troubles. All your focus is on those difficulties and as long as you keep your focus on the difficulties, they will compound and become bigger and worse with time. Putting your whole attention on the problems only communicates to the universe, that you want more of those problems. And life or the universe will have no option than to serve you more of whatever you are going through.

"Identity is a prison you can never escape, but the way to redeem your past is not to run from it, but to try to understand it, and use it as a foundation to grow."
~ Jay-Z

You kind of like it because you are not really taking initiative or actions to solve them. You are just waiting for the government's interventions in cash or kind. You are waiting for your brother, sister, parents, etc., to come save you. Some of us are just waiting for Jesus Christ, God or whatever deity we believe in to come to our aid from heaven or something. Why do we have to wait for Jesus Christ, God or whatever deity we believe in to come and save us from our troubles when we have been created in the image and likeness of God; having similar power and authority to effect positive changes in our lives? Is it not written in Psalms 82:6 that 'ye are gods and children of the Most-High'? What then happened to the gods and children of the Most-High?

*"...I am amazed at how this **great wealth** has made its home in this poverty."*
~ Words of Jesus Christ according to the Book of Thomas vs. 29.

Do you by chance understand what Jesus Christ meant by "this great wealth"? That is, you and I as gods. Our spirit-souls are the great wealth that have made its home in "this poverty". Where "this poverty" refers to the flesh or body. In making our homes in 'this poverty', we have lost touch with ourselves, the true us; our divine identity, our spirit-souls and we have taken on this illusory self-identity of the body or the flesh with its limitations. We have lost touch of our grandness as divine beings incarnated in flesh. We are yet to discover the immeasurable values and potentials of our spirit-souls. Had we known or re-membered of our true values and essence, we wouldn't be suffering and struggling as a sentient race on Earth.

We go to church, visit the mosques and shrines alright but how many of us are truly connected to our spirit-souls? If we were indeed deeply and truly connected to our divine state, we wouldn't sit around for our lives to be ordered and determined by the *men in high castles* or by the happenstances of life. Eyes have not seen nor did ears hear of the true essence of the human spirit-soul; its immeasurable qualities and potentials. We are more than what we have been told or taught to believe and accept as true over the millennial. We are far more than eyes can meet. [2]Even evidence from scientific studies of the human DNA validates this, that we are gods in flesh. In one of his researches about the human origin and DNA, a scientist by name Gregg Braden came to a stunning conclusion. The first level of information decoded from the human DNA translated as *"God Eternal within the Body*". This information was encoded in our DNAs by our creator/creators. We are gods incarnated within a body. And we should live as such. You can find more about this intriguing research finding via the link provided in the reference page.

> *"All life is an experiment. The more experiments you make, the better."*
> ~ *Ralph Waldo Emerson*

All Things Are Working Together For Your Becoming

"If life were predictable it would cease to be life, and be without flavor."
~ Eleanor Roosevelt

Life with its experiences can sometimes be confounding, in the sense that in moving from a high energetic state (spiritual state) to lower energetic state (inhabiting the body at birth), we lose a lot of our spiritual energies. Our bodies at its current state of evolution or development cannot contain all of our immense spiritual energies. Therefore, when we are given birth to, we have very little to no option than to lose or shrink down from the high energetic state so that we can inhabit the human body. And this process takes a toll on our spirituality. We become subjected to somewhat total spiritual amnesia. We kind of forget who we are as gods or part of the divineness of the universe, by some intricate process unknown to us. We forget where we came from, the multiple lives we have lived in the past, the multiple lives we are still living (multiverse theory), via various unknown spiritual processes, and our oneness with everyone and everything else in the universe and beyond, etc.

"The big lesson in life, baby, is never be scared of anyone or anything."
~ Frank Sinatra.

When we come anew to this physical plane (lower state), we have to constantly and frequently be nourishing our high energetic state (spiritual state) via sleep. The very reason why babies tend to sleep a lot. This is because they have to keep connecting or going back to the spiritual state to receive of more energy to compensate for the sudden loss of energy or change of state brought about by inhabiting the body. For years we have been told that we sleep so that our bodies can receive rest and regeneration in the sleep state. And this is true to a point. But another less known reason why we sleep is to reconnect our spirits to the universal divine state for spiritual energy recharge. Anytime the spirit-soul of an individual realizes that it is wearing out or have no immediate task in the physical plane, it induces the body to go into a state of rest, so that it can reconnect to the eternal spiritual source for recharge. This high energetic state recharge is necessary so that the spirit-soul can continue to live on the physical plane.

When we transition from our higher energetic state to the lower energetic state, we lose a lot of our essence; of who we are as spiritual entities. To explain further, let me borrow from the diction of atomic and nuclei physics. An atom is made up of a center called nucleus, with electrons orbiting around it. These electrons occupy different energy levels around the nucleus. We have some that orbit close to the nucleus and others orbit far away from the nucleus; on the atomic scale. When an electron moves from a higher state (far from the nucleus) to a lower state (close to the nucleus), it loses energy to the surrounding in the form of light or electromagnetic wave. At the lower state, because the electron has lost its essence (high energy), it will behave as if it belongs with the lower state electrons. It will act and behave as the lower state electrons do. If this electron doesn't receive any energy boost to shoot it back to its original high energy state, it will become trapped in the lower orbit or energy state forever. If this electron is to receive energy boost in the form of heat or any other electromagnetic wave, it can gain energy and remember whence it came from; the high energy state, and move there accordingly.

"The way I see it, if you want the rainbow, you gotta put up with the rain."
~ Dolly Parton

I am theorizing in this book that this phenomenon doesn't just occur to atoms or at the atomic state only. It seeps into the macro world like in the spirit to physical realm transition. Just like an electron loses energy when it moves from the higher orbital state to a lower orbital state, the human spirit-soul likewise loses a chunk of its energy, in order to allow it to inhabit the body. The spirit-soul inhabiting a body can become lost in the physical plane. It can lose a lot of its energy to the point that it would forget about itself entirely. When this happens, the spirit-soul needs to be reminded of itself and its essence. And this is what is popularly known in Christian parlance as being born again. It has mainly got to do with the reactivation of the spirit-soul's energy; reconnecting it to its Divine Self, aka God/Allah.

Though our spirit-souls get nourishment from the spiritual world during sleep, it is not enough to help it maintain its position in its originally high energetic state. It needs more than just sleep to able to return to its original high energy state of being. This more addition can come about by prayer, meditation, worship, shamanic activities and other related positive spiritual practices. By practicing these activities, we consciously push our spiritual energies aka anointing, from the lower state of being to a higher state of being. Like an electron in an atomic structure that can be energized to higher orbital levels, we can energize our spirit-souls via these practices, to a higher state of being or consciousness. Interestingly, there is no limit to how high we can go or attain in our state of being. We can go as high as we want to, because there is no limit to the Divine Self, aka God.

> *"Everything negative – pressure, challenges – is all an opportunity for me to rise."*
> *~ Kobe Bryant*

Though most of us don't retain a lot of our spiritual energies when we transit to this earthly plane, few people often have enough residual energies from their transitions to the point that they are able to remember having lived past lives. Some are able to reconnect with past life forms in their current life forms and some do remember almost every other aspect of them living in the multiverse plane of existence. As to how these few individuals do have memory of past and multiple lives, and the rest of us don't have any trace or clue to these events ever happening to us, is something that at the moment I have no knowledge of. I can hypothesize that whatever body these few individuals inhabit is strong enough to contain extra spiritual residual energies from past or multiple lives lived.

"Do not dwell in the past, do not dream of the future, concentrate the mind on the present moment."
~ Buddha

Nothing Really Matters

"Life is not a problem to be solved, but a reality to be experienced."
~ Soren Kierkegaard

Why are we here on earth? What is it that we are doing in the cosmos? In effect all life is about, is experiencing ourselves; who we are as gods or as beings of high celestial importance or essence. All that matters in this journey called life is to finally return to our higher energetic state of being. In coming to this earth, we forget who we are in order to remember who we are as sentient beings of immense power; to experience our all-powerfulness. All our woes and cries only serve as a means for us to remember who we are. All our troubles and temptations are all set by ourselves together with the Divine Source, to help us find our way home; back to the Source of All Things.

On the physical plane, a lot can matter to us. This is because our brains or minds have to find a way to make sense of whatever we are going through, whether good or bad. But on the spiritual level, we somewhat know very well that nothing really matters. Whatever we go through are just experiential moments in space-time continuum. Moments that will eventually pass into the "no-thingness" state. If we were to understand life from this perspective that every moment of our lives are experiential moments in space-time, nothing would really worry us and you would enjoy life to its maximum whether we go through good times or bad times. We would know that the universe has got our backs whether things go south or not. The levels of stress related sicknesses and death would drop drastically.

"Never take life seriously. Nobody gets out alive anyway."
~ Anonymous

Our inability to retain a lot of our spiritual energies when we transit to this physical plane, makes us susceptible to effects and characteristics associated with lower vibrational spiritual energies. These lower vibrational energies include but not limited to fear, anger, anxiety, jealousy, hatred, selfishness, stress, etc. That is why it is very important for us to reconnect with our Source, once we transit to this world and we become conscious of who we are. Reconnecting with the Source gives us the energy boost to rise above the lower vibrational energies and their effect on us emotionally and spiritually.

No matter what you are going through whether good or otherwise, know and understand that everything is going together for your becoming. Don't curse the bad days and bless the good ones. Know that all things are working together for your good. If the bad you are going through, after your careful analysis, is your own creation, it is in your power to change your fate. If whatever you are going through stems from your spirit-soul's journey or path of evolution, then enjoy the process while it last, knowing very well that nothing can really hurt you or destroy you. I mean the real you; your spirit-soul. Enjoy the process of becoming the god you were created to be, from before time began. And no matter what happens to you at each step of the way, the universe has got your back. Just keep on living and experiencing yourself in all the ways that life will afford you.

"Live for each second without hesitation"
~ Elton John

References

1. The Unconscious Mind: https://m.youtube.com/watch?v=a2MSc3eNS1Y&t=45s. Date accessed: January, 2020.
2. 'God Eternal within the Body': https://m.youtube.com/watch?v=_dcup7NG_b0. Date accessed: October, 2019.

THE END